# YOUR FUTURE IS WRITTEN
## *IN THE STARS!*

With the help of Sydney Omarr's expert readings, 1987 will be your best year ever. Whatever you desire can be yours if you look to the stars for guidance—*now* is the time to fulfill your most daring dreams!

This expert astrologer's time-tested wisdom shows you how to turn your fantasies into exciting realities. You'll learn all about the key numbers in your life, the days that are most favorable to your goals, and all the other important information you need to chart your way straight to the top in 1987!

# SYDNEY OMARR'S

## DAY-BY-DAY ASTROLOGICAL GUIDE FOR

*Scorpio*

# 1 · 9 · 8 · 7

( OCTOBER 23–NOVEMBER 21 )

A SIGNET BOOK

**NEW AMERICAN LIBRARY**

SIGNET TRADEMARK REG. U.S. PAT. OFF. AND FOREIGN COUNTRIES
REGISTERED TRADEMARK—MARCA REGISTRADA
HECHO EN CHICAGO, U.S.A.

SIGNET, SIGNET CLASSIC, MENTOR, PLUME, MERIDIAN AND NAL BOOKS
are published by New American Library,
1633 Broadway, New York, New York 10019

First Printing, July, 1986

1  2  3  4  5  6  7  8  9

PRINTED IN THE UNITED STATES OF AMERICA

# CONTENTS

# Introduction 1987—
# Making the Most of It!

What makes a great year? Happiness, success, good fortune in large doses—this might be your *immediate* answer. But think a moment. Isn't a truly satisfying, memorable year *also* one when you make the most of everything that comes your way; when you stretch yourself and grow mentally, emotionally, and professionally; when you develop deep, lasting, and productive relationships with others?

Some of those happy and fortunate events may be fated in the stars, but astrology teaches that the good times can have just as much to do with free will—with how you pick and choose among the options available in every situation. In fact, you can create much of your own good fortune by using astrology as a tool to help you first discover the range of possibilities at any given time and then deciding which among them would be the most advantagous course of action.

Astrology provides you with different "road

maps" with signposts, detours, and exit markings to guide you. One is your horoscope, based on the planetary configuration on the day you were born. The special energies that were happening at that moment are full of clues about your personality and potential, about what avenues for you to explore, what talents to develop, who will be your best partner, and how to deal with life's challenges.

On another level, astrology is an understanding of the energies of the universe, the way the planetary forces are interacting at any given time. This is another road map that can help you make a timetable for putting your plans into action. You may have noticed that, at certain times, you feel drawn in a particular direction; that there are times when everything seems to go smoothly, or conversely, when everything (and everyone) seems out of sorts. Astrology explains that a moment in time is the product of many forces, many energies that can harmonize or conflict. Understanding these forces and how and when to use them can help you keep your balance, get over the rough spots, and make the good times even better. This book will give you the exact dates when you have the green light to go after what you want in your career, in your love life, and in your routine daily chores.

The more you know about astrology, the more you'll appreciate its practical techniques. It can help you with such everyday problems as when to buy and sell, when to stay out of the action, when to decorate your home, when to start an exercise program, and even when you will be most attractive to everyone you meet. It can also point out when it's time to stop and reflect, to get away from it all, to recharge your energies.

The most fascinating aspect of astrology for most people is the insights it gives into relationships with others, the startlingly accurate and useful imformation about your friends, family, lovers, employers. It shows how to please them, how to attract a love and make it last, how to deal with each sign's particular foibles. It shows how to harmonize with others and how and when to compromise. It points to better ways of dealing with people and to achieving happier solutions to conflicts.

The best news is that you don't have to be a professional astrologer to understand and use astrology practically and positively in your life. This book will show you many ways you can use astrology immediately.

It starts with the basics ... the language and ideas that have kept the study of this field fascinating since ancient times. You'll get a well-rounded, overall picture that takes the mystery out of astrology and will hopefully give you a new appreciation of this intriguing field.

Then it deals with your personal astrological portrait. You'll discover new sides of yourself through your sun sign and what it reveals about your talents, drives, ups and downs. How your rising sign affects the way you appear to the rest of the world. What the moon and planetary cycles can mean to you. How you can have better relationships with others.

Finally, this book gives you a day-by-day timetable for action, showing exactly where the moon is, how this relates to your life, and the forces to work with every day of the year.

So let this guide be a tool to help you make this the most productive, successful year ever—in all areas of your life!

# 1

## The Basics—
## Understanding the Sun Signs

### How Astrology Began

What exactly *is* astrology many of us ask? Is it superstition? Is it a religion? Is it fortune-telling? Is it a craft? An art? A science?

Astrology is actually man's first way of understanding himself, of relating his own complex nature to the cosmic order of the universe.

Astrology was once the same as astronomy; both came from man's fascination with the changes in the heavens. Early star-gazers noticed that certain heavenly bodies stayed fixed in constellations, while others moved in the sky. Then they observed that the movements of these "planets" seemed to coincide with specific kinds of events here on earth, from major conflicts such as wars, to happenings of nature like floods and earthquakes, to everyday human behavior—love, birth, quarrels, travels. As the early astrologers carefully observed the sun, moon, and planets, they concluded that the positions of certain heavenly bodies at the birth of a person (or a country, or a business, or an event) can affect that person's character and later development. This hypothesis became the central assumption of astrology.

The word "astrology" comes from the Greek word for star, "astron," and "logos" meaning discourse.

However, the two fields of astrology and astronomy split as astrologers became concerned with divination and prediction and speculations about human destiny, while astronomers relegated themselves to strictly scientific observation.

Because many unscrupulous practitioners and charlatans used astrology for their own purposes, the craft became fraught with superstition. It was banned by the Christian church in 1550, later outlawed in England in 1736 under the Witchcraft Act, and generally discredited until the early 1900s when it began, once more, to be taken seriously.

Today, there are still many controversies about astrology, but serious professional astrologers have banded together in organizations that maintain strict standards. They are trained in a rigorous discipline, involving highly technical observations and calculations. So the reputation of astrology as a thoughtful interpretive craft is growing. It is a subject that manages to be both humanistic and scientific, both intuitive and exacting, and endlessly alluring to everyone who is interested in the complexities of the universe as they relate to human nature.

# The Zodiac—Planetary Highway

As the planets are observed in the sky, from our vantage point on earth, they seem to wander along a certain path through the heavens. This path has been known since ancient times as the zodiac, which means "circle of animals," because many of the constellations on the path have names of animals or sea creatures—Aries the ram, Cancer the crab; leo the lion, Taurus the bull, etc. Astrologers divide this circle of the zodiac around the sky (with earth as the central reference point) into 30-degree segments because, as the sun appears to "move" along the path, it passes through each segment in about 30 days.

Each of these segments of the zodiac path is named for a constellation, which acts as a handy reference point. However, you may note that the signs along the pathway of the zodiac do not necessarily correspond with the exact locations of their namesake constellations. Because the earth's axis has changed through the centuries since astrology began, the position of the constellations along the path has also shifted, so "Aquarius" for instance is in a different place on the zodiac than it was centuries ago. But the 30-degree segment of the zodiac named after Aquarius remains the same, even though the constellation has moved.

On the zodiac highway, the sun takes one year to travel through all the twelve segments or "signs." When it is traveling through a particular sign, those born at that time are born under the influence of that sign. That is what we call a sun sign.

If you were born while the sun was passing through the Gemini segment of the highway, you are a "Gemini." Nine other planets will be passing through other signs at the same time, but it is the sun that determines your basic astrological personality. It is the most important astral body in your horoscope. The others have important, but lesser, meaning for you.

## What Kind of Sun Sign Are You?

Each sign has a very special character of its own that is quite different from the sign preceding or following it. What causes this difference? Several factors: its *element* or basic personality; the way it operates or its *quality*; and its positive or negative *polarity* which also corresponds to its masculine or feminine sex. These three classifications—*element, quality,* and *polarity*—combine to give each sign a blend of different forces which interact with each other to make the sign unique.

### Element

The signs were first classified by the four *elements: fire, earth, air,* and *water*, which ancients believed made up everything and everybody. Astrologers believe the elements explain the way each sign experiences life, so each sign was assigned an element. Starting with Aries, which became the first fire sign, the elements follow with earth, air, and water in that same sequence repeated throughout the twelve signs.

- The fire signs are Aries, Leo, and Sagittarius.
- The earth signs are Taurus, Virgo, and Capricorn.
- The air signs are Gemini, Libra, and Aquarius.
- The water signs are Cancer, Scorpio, and Pisces.

The element of fire starts the cycle of the zodiac with Aries. Fire spreads light, energy, warmth, excitement. So it follows that people born under the fire signs are people of action, sharing, the most dynamic, optimistic, and energetic signs of the zodiac. Fire signs are impatient, passionate, daring. They have strong wills and hot tempers. They love to take the spotlight and to make ideas come to life.

Earth signs follow through, after fire's energetic push, making things happen in the material world. For earth signs, "seeing is believing,"—so is hearing, touching, smelling, and tasting. These signs are the realists of the zodiac. They provide sustenance, stability, continuity. They stand for the solid and practical. Earth signs care about how things work. They are sensualists who live in and enjoy the things of the world.

The air signs are the communicators of the zodiac. They spread the word. They represent all that is mental, sociable, versatile. These signs help us explore human intelligence—the mental world of ideas and concepts. They are the original thinkers who inspire us through their use of words, color, style, and beauty. They need human contact and thrive on discussion, debate, and charm. They enjoy the mental world.

The water signs live in the world of feelings. Water is the element of emotions and compassion; here are the imaginative intuitive thinkers—the poets and artists of the zodiac. These are the non-verbal communicators, who have uncanny perceptions. They are the sensitive mystics of the zodiac, fascinated by the mysteries of life.

**Quality**      The *quality* of a sign tells you how it operates. There are *three* different qualities: the first is *cardinal*—which are the signs of action, Aries, Cancer, Libra, and Capricorn. The second quality is *fixed*, the signs of stability: Taurus, Leo, Scorpio, and Aquarius. And the third represents the signs of change, the *mutables:* Gemini, Virgo, Sagittarius, and Pisces.

*Cardinal Signs Start Things Up.*      The cardinal signs are the spark plugs of the zodiac. They set the other signs in motion. Aries starts the spring season, it is the first sign of the zodiac and, propelled by the element of fire, the most energetic. Cancer starts the summer season; it is the most active and moody of the water signs. Libra starts the fall season; it is the air sign that works actively to create harmony, justice, and peace. Capricorn brings on winter and is the most aggressive organizer of the earth signs.

*The Fixed Signs Stand for Stability.*      These are the signs that are the builders. After the start-up energy of the cardinal signs, their work is to settle and stabilize, to plant themselves and grow. They represent the middle or height of each season:

Thus Taurus brings the spring season into full bloom, Leo comes at the height of summer, Scorpio the harvest of fall, and Aquarius the fullness of the winter season.

***The Mutable Signs Represent Change and Transformation.*** These are the flexible signs of the zodiac, which prepare each season for change. The mutable signs are the chameleons of the zodiac, the versatile people who have the ability to adjust easily to different circumstances. So the sparkling, witty Gemini takes spring into summer, the analytical Virgo takes summer into fall, the always-on-the-move Sagittarius heralds the end of fall, and the romantic, emotional Pisces closes the winter season, preparing the way for cardinal Aries to give birth to spring.

**Polarity ... The Yin and Yang of the Zodiac** The third way of classifying signs is by whether they are masculine and "positive" or feminine and "negative." The zodiac is divided into masculine and feminine signs, starting with a masculine sign, Aries, and alternating masculine and feminine through the twelve signs. As it turns out, all the fire and air signs are masculine, and all the earth and water signs are feminine.

*Masculine "Positive" Signs:* Aries, Leo, Sagittarius, Gemini, Libra, Aquarius.

*Feminine "Negative" signs:* Taurus, Virgo, Capricorn, Cancer, Scorpio, Pisces.

The masculine signs are more outer directed, more straightforward, more "yang"; the feminine

17

signs tend to be more introspective, more subtly attuned to the subconscious, more "yin."

Each sign complements and leads into the next sign, making a voyage around the zodiac like a voyage through the realms of human experience, starting with the energy of birth in Aries and ending with the accumulated wisdom of Pisces. Here is how it works.

The masculine get-up-and-go of Aries starts off the trip, leading into the slower feminine nurturing and flowering of Taurus. Then the verbal powers of masculine Gemini reach out into the world. The warm sensitive feminine Cancer adds feeling and caring, gives a "home" to the restless Gemini energy. Then this energy goes on securely to take the leadership role given by masculine Leo.

Feminine Virgo reflects and analyzes the working operation with a critical eye, correcting and perfecting, changing it for the better. It next aquires logical perspective and a balance of inner and outer forces from masculine Libra. But Libra tends to operate on the surface, resisting decisions until Scorpio's inner-directed feminine intensity probes deeply and decisively, to gain control. The serious Scorpio can be a bit heavy, however; so the optimism of outgoing Sagittarius is welcome. Masculine Sagittarius is a salesman, but it takes feminine Capricorn to close the deal and give the operation a solid organization. Aquarius uplifts the goals with lofty ideals, humanitarian aims, and the journey is finally completed by feminine Pisces, which sums up the wisdom accumulted so far and adds the emotions and feelings. Thus the circle starts again with Aries.

What happens if you are born with your sun in a sign not of your own sex? It hardly means that you are more or less of a "man" or "woman." Depending on the position of the rest of the planets at that time, it simply means that you have a special balance of energies available to you. As you learn the placements of the rest of the planets in your horoscope, study the positives and negatives for some real insight into your special astrological persona. Too many planets placed in "positive" signs may indicate a need for reflective thinking—you may have to guard against having too much going on at once and spreading yourself too thin. Too many "negatives" may indicate a lack of get up and go. You may need to get out of yourself and into the world.

## How It All Adds Up . . . The Portrait of Each Sign

The sum-up of each sign is like a recipe made up of several variable ingredients. Each has its own flavor based on the blending of element, quality, and polarity. Here is how they mix:

*Aries—March 21–April 19*
Element: Fire      Quality: Cardinal
Polarity: Masculine/positive

The dash, energy, and headstrong impetuousness of this sign comes from the dynamic fire element propelled by the action-ready cardinal quality and masculine polarity. No wonder this is one of the most impatient and unstoppable signs, always anxious to get there first! It is also the trend-setter of the zodiac.

### Taurus—April 20–May 20
Element: Earth     Quality: Fixed
Polarity: Feminine/negative

Along comes Taurus to stop and think things over. Its fixed earth character is anxious to build things that last. It has a superabundance of patience, and a great desire to nurture others as well as an appreciation of material things and the beauties of the "earth." Most Taureans are natural gardeners, the "green thumbs" of the zodiac.

### Gemini—May 21–June 21
Element: Air     Quality: Mutable
Polarity: Masculine/positive

Verbal Gemini is forever changing its mind and often tries to do two things at once. Its function as dictated by mutable air is to communicate ideas. As a positive masculine sign, it is extremely extroverted and sociable and loves to get people out of a static rut. Geminis are the charmers of the zodiac, never at a loss for words.

### Cancer—June 22–July 22
Element: Water     Quality: Cardinal
Polarity: Feminine/negative

As a cardinal water sign, Cancer can turn its feelings into productive use. Cancers often excel through using their water sign intuition and nurturing qualities in business and creative fields. Though they often appear shy and sensitive, they can quietly be a very active and powerful force. They are also known for their maternal instincts. Even male Cancers love to "mother" others.

### Leo—July 23–August 22
Element: Fire    Quality: Fixed
Polarity: Masculine/positive

The fixed fire of Leo burns with a steady and powerful flame. This positive sign loves to be noticed and to take the lead, to be the strong sign others lean on and look up to. Their fixed passions plus their positive enthusiasms make this a sign to be reckoned with. Leos always take center stage; even quiet Leos have "presence."

### Virgo—August 23–September 22
Element: Earth    Quality: Mutable
Polarity: Feminine/negative

Virgo combines the practicality of earth, the nurturing feminine polarity, and the mutable sense of change. It adds up to an analytical sign that desires to be of service to others. Virgo adjusts to the material changes of life—attempting to sort them out so they will run smoothly. The perfection of practical things, the organization many ever-present details of life, and the maintenance of high standards are Virgo's concerns.

### Libra—September 23–October 23
Element: Air    Quality: Cardinal
Polarity: Masculine/positive

Libra combines the intellectual and judgmental nature of air with a positive action-oriented character. Libra is a debater, a diplomat who can juggle people and ideas and work actively to create justice, harmony, and beauty in the environment.

### Scorpio—October 24–November 21
Element: Water    Quality: Fixed
Polarity: Feminine/negative

Scorpio's powerful fixed water nature gives this sign the deepest emotions and the desire to control and contain them. Its nurturing feminine side gives them the intense desire to probe innermost reaches of the psyche, to get to the root of matters to solve problems. Scorpios are the detectives of the zodiac.

### Sagittarius—November 22–December 21
Element: Fire    Quality: Mutable
Polarity: Masculine/positive

In Sagittarius, the mutable fire element plus the masculine positive force project great energy and enthusiasm, both mentally and physically. Sagittarians often express this physically, becoming star athletes or becoming supersalesmen or politicians or spiritual leaders who ignite with all the flame of their enthusiasm and energy. They are always on the move and love to spread their ideas around.

### Capricorn—December 22–January 19
Element: Earth    Quality: Cardinal
Polarity: Feminine/negative

Because Capricorn is an active earth sign that likes to see material results, it is often known as the achiever of the zodiac. This is the conservative sign that runs the show behind the scenes. It nurtures others by providing the organizational umbrella to shelter them. With Capricorn, things happen.

### Aquarius—January 20–February 19
Element: Air    Quality: Fixed
Polarity: Masculine/positive

The fixed air of Aquarius gives this sign high ideals and makes them search out universal truths and ways to project them for the betterment of mankind. The active, masculine positive polarity of Aquarians helps them understand the power of fame and how to use it to espouse worthy causes—a good reason why they are known for their political ability and for their innate sense of how to use the media.

### Pisces—February 20–March 20
Element: Water    Quality: Mutable
Polarity: Feminine/negative

The mutable ever-moving water of Pisces gives great intuitive understanding of emotions. It is a sign that knows no emotional boundaries; it does not judge, but can sympathize with everyone. It needs to find a nurturing outlet for its emotions, one that speaks to mankind. Then it can use the accumulated wisdom of the zodiac creatively.

## How Do the Signs get Along Together? It's Element-al!

"How does my sign get along with others?" This is a question astrologers hear more than any other.

Or it can go something like: "I'm a Cancer and my boyfriend is a Libra . . . is this the right sign for me?"

The answer is usually "Well, yes and no. It depends on many factors." A comparison of any two *complete* horoscopes, with all the ten planetary placements taken into consideration, is the best way to evaluate a relationship in detail. You might have the sun in Cancer and the moon in Libra or Venus in Capricorn, all of which can be compared with the placements in the other person's horoscope.

But an easy and fast way to get an overview of the relationship is to compare the sun sign elements. Though this will not give you specific details, it can give you important clues about the ways you relate to each other, what you have to offer each other, and where you may have to compromise or adjust. You can use the knowledge you have learned so far about the signs.

First, bear in mind that there are no "good" or "bad" combinations in the zodiac. A relationship between two people of the same sun sign may be very compatible . . . but you might find yourself a bit bored in time, perhaps craving someone with a bit more dynamism. Since most of us look for a mate who is interesting as well as compatible, we are often attracted to those whose elements provide enough contrast and stimulation, who show us sides of experience other than the ones so familiar to us.

Here's a recap of the signs in each element. For a moment, think of yourself—and the person who attracts you—as embodying the elements of your respective sun signs. The sun's element will color your horoscope most, even though you will certainly have planets placed in other elements:

*Fire:* Aries, Leo, Sagittarius
*Earth:* Taurus, Virgo, Capricorn
*Air:* Gemini, Libra, Aquarius
*Water:* Cancer, Scorpio, Pisces

You get important clues to what the elements do to and for each other in relationships if you look to the physical world, just as if you were in a chemistry laboratory. The interactions of the signs have many parallels to what occurs in the natural world. We learn from and teach our lovers in the ways we nurture or conflict with each other's chemistry. Each sign must find a good chemical balance with the other elements to grow and reach its full potential in any relationship.

## How the Fire signs Relate

Earth can fuel fire's flame or smother it. Fire signs who are drawn to earth signs will find a partner who can help them accomplish their goals and keep their flame on a steady course. However earth's possessiveness and love of material things may curb fire's natural wanderlust. Fire loves to be the boss, to keep its options open! The challenge is to *use* the strong base of operations that earth provides to make more exciting fire ventures possible. And fire must understand that earth needs roots—all the bills paid and a strong home base.

Air can cause fire to burn more brightly, but too much fire can just mean a lot of hot air.

Nothing gets done! And much energy gets dissipated. Fire's passionate spirit blends well with air's logical mind. And you ignite each other physically.

Water can put a damper on fire's energy. It can literally rain on the parade. Or together they can bring things to a boil and create a lot of steam. Water's creativity inspires fire to great heights of excitement and drama. And the sensitive emotions of water can stoke fire's ego. They know instinctively how to make you feel good (they also know how to dampen your spirit). Fire can tune in to the fantasy of water and give them the confidence to live it out. But the challenge will be for fire to deal with the sensitive feelings of water, to develop compassion and sympathy for others. Tact is not fire's strong point.

Fire with fire is either a conflagration or a competition—or total burnout. Since fire does not like to compromise, this could be too much of a good thing, with both signs going their separate ways in short order.

**How the Earth Signs Relate**
Earth signs, who often tend to be slow starters, are often fascinated by the dynamism of the fire element. They in turn provide the follow through, the organization and attention to detail that fire signs usually lack. If they can curb their possessiveness and not smother the enthusiasm of fire or try to cage these volatile people, the relationship can be productive.

Earth and air need much give and take. Initially, they may not seem to have much in common. Earth is concerned with the physical, while Air is interested in mental stimulation. The warm earth signs may not understand the cool air sign's detachment. But earth can add a sense of reality to air signs, which can turn them into do-ers as well as thinkers and can give them substance. Much depends on how willing both are to give and take.

Earth and water have many natural affinities. Earth loves to take care of water, while water's caring and creativity can make earth flower. A water sign also understands and blends beautifully with earth signs' sensuality. But sometimes, too much down-to-earth realism can smother the water signs' creativity and depress them emotionally. Then there's a flood and mud.

Two earth signs could be super productive together or bury each other! These signs need stimulation to get going and too much earth could result in a stick-in-the-mud relationship.

## How Air Signs Relate

Air signs and fire signs might be ideal for each other. Fire gives air power, which air can use to spread the word on fire's enthusiastic schemes. However too much air can blow them away with logic. It's fine if air can fan the flame, not blow it out!

With earth signs, air has to reckon with their physical needs. These are signs of action, not talk, that want to see results and get down to business. Air signs may find this cramps their style. They like to socialize, to experiment with ideas and people, while earth signs like to cultivate their own gardens. The partnership depends on how well air's ideas and ideals mesh with earth signs' ambitions and goals.

Air may not really want to deal with water signs' emotions . . . at first. But water's natural creativity can exert a tremendous attraction. Water gives depth to air's ideas and can bring a new level of understanding and perception to their brilliant logic and communicative skills.

Two air signs can be breezy companions or blow each other away with all talk and no action. You will spend much time debating problems and not enough time solving them.

## How Water Signs Relate

Water is naturally harmonious with earth and welcomes its discipline and nurturing as well as its organizational ability, which can give shape to their creative ideas. Water truly inspires earth to get moving in productive ways. Both signs seem not to mind each other's possessiveness. However, it is materialism that is the villain here. Too much practicality can dry up water's source of inspiration. While too much soggy emotionalism can erode earth's sense of purpose.

Water and fire create great energy together, but this combination is always a challenge. Fire has a powerful ego that can ride roughshod over tender sensitive feelings. Watery tears can quickly drown fire's enthusiasm. The key is to find goals you both believe in, where fire can promote water's talents, and water can reflect fire's flame.

Water and air work well together when water's inspiration and creativity is heightened by air sign's logic and perspective. Air can lift water's dark moods, give them bouyancy, and take them out into the world. If air can understand water's need for emotional reassurance and Water can give air room to breathe—and not stifle them with possessiveness—the match can work.

Water and water can either have the deepest emotional bliss or drown each other. Much depends on how they harness and blend their talents and perceptions. This can be a very spiritual relationship, with a communication on deep unspoken levels.

### Do "Opposites Attract" In Astrology . . . or Are You Better Off With the "Sign Next Door"?

Another way of looking at relationships is to see in what position the other person's sign is located in reference to your own sign. As we have mentioned before, the signs of the zodiac are marked off in 30-degree segments. Signs that are next door to each other on the wheel are considered fairly compatible . . . but the chemistry is not usually intense. There is an air of good fellowship, a brother–sister attraction rather than a grand passion. Signs that are two signs apart (60 degrees) are very good together. You're far enough away for there to be real interest. Signs that are four signs away are also considered good. However these will be signs in the same element, which might be too much of a good thing.

The challenging positions are signs with the *same*

*quality* (cardinal, fixed, or mutable) but *different elements*. These can be signs that are 180 degrees apart, directly opposite each other on the circular zodiac path. (This can work or not work depending on whether "opposites attract.")

Signs that are 90 degrees, or three signs away from each other, are said to be in square aspect. These are the most challenging and stimulating relationships. You operate in the same way, but with different equipment. One thing is certain: Signs in the square aspect are rarely bored with each other.

Some combinations of signs work better for friendships—where mutual stimulation is the goal; others for love affairs—where passion is kindled and nurtured; others for marriage, which requires deep commitment, compromise, and mutual understanding. However, there is no ideal combination of signs and elements. Many people who have successful relationships love each other because each provides elements that the other is missing and needs. Then there are relationships between "soul mates" of the same element and often the same sign. They can read each other's minds and thoughts. But, once more, there are no hard and fast rules. Any combination can work together if you understand and can accept what the other sign needs and offers—and vice versa.

To prove this point, here is a list of famous happy couples, who have found seventh heaven together in spite of so-called "unfavorable" sun-sign combinations. In some cases, other planetary aspects may have outweighed elemental differences. In others, it was an undeniable chemical attraction.

### Some Lovers with Their Signs "Next Door"

Mick Jagger (Leo) and Jerry Hall (Cancer)

Paul Newman (Aquarius) and Joanne Woodward (Pisces)

The late Duke and Duchess of Windsor (Cancer and Gemini)

Phil Donahue (Sagittarius) and Marlo Thomas (Scorpio)

### These Happy Lovers Have Sun Signs "Squaring Off"

John Derek (Leo) and Bo Derek (Scorpio)

Frank Sinatra (Sagittarius) and Barbara Sinatra (Pisces)

Cliff Robertson (Virgo) and Dina Merrill (Sagittarius)

Harry S. Truman (Taurus) and Bess Truman (Aquarius)

### Here Are Some "Opposites" Who Attracted ... and Married

Candice Bergen (Taurus) and Louis Malle (Scorpio)

Helen Gurley Brown (Aquarius) and David Brown (Leo)

Simone Signoret (Aries) and Yves Montand (Libra)

### Some "Odd Elements" Who Matched Up

Ronald Reagan (Aquarius) and Nancy (Cancer)

Gerald Ford (Cancer) and Betty (Aries)

Robert Kennedy (Scorpio) and Ethel (Aries)

Juan Peron (Libra) and Evita (Taurus)

George Washington (Pisces) and Martha (Gemini)

# 2

## The Horoscope:
## Your Personal Map of the Heavens

Looking for the first time at a horoscope drawn up by an astrologer, you'll see a strange chart that looks like a wheel decorated with odd symbols, numbers, and geometric shapes. It is hard to believe that this chart, seemingly written in a language from outer space, can tell so much about your career, your hopes, your intimate love life! And even more astonishing is the fact that no two horoscopes are exactly alike, even if you are one of twins born moments apart. Your horoscope is as much "you" as your fingerprint: it's a look at your life from a special vantage point that can be achieved no other way.

A horoscope is really a "picture" of a specific moment in time, as seen from a particular spot on earth, looking at the heavens. It actually shows where the sun, moon, and other eight planets are traveling on the zodiac pathway at that very moment.

Astrologers draw up horoscopes for the moment of time when something is born. Whether it is a person, a business, a country, a love affair, or even a question to be answered, everything that has a moment of beginning can have a horoscope. Going back to the basic astrological theory that everything embodies a moment in time, this map of the heavens is drawn up to reveal exactly what the qualities of that moment *are,* so the astrologer can advise the subject of the horoscope how to use these qualities.

Though one can tell much from the position of the sun in a chart, astrologers will look at many other relationships in the horoscope, such as the position of the moon and planets, what sign they are in and how they relate to each other. They'll also determine which sign is on the horizon at the moment of birth; this affects where the planets are located above or below the horizon. Finally, they'll consider how the horoscope relates to what is happening at the *present moment* in the sky.

## How an Astrologer Looks at the Planets

Planets are important to the astrologer for two reasons. First, the *sign* of each planet contributes to the total *personality* of the subject of the horoscope. Then, the planets' paths through the zodiac every day or year or lifetime indicate events as they will happen in the course of the subject's life.

If planets were just anonymous moving bodies in the sky, they would mean little to us. However, at some point in time, planets became personalities. They acquired "star quality." Some were good guys, some were sexy, some were hot-tempered. Then they started to get involved with us. Certain events in the sky seemed to coincide with a certain type of event on earth. In fact, planets were once thought to rule people's lives to such an extent that they were considered gods. Many cultures worshiped the sun and moon as givers of life. The sun was usually male and the moon female, such as Diana or Artemis. Jupiter was the good guy who brought luck and abundance. But Saturn became the stern fatherly disciplinarian who tested us and reminded us of our duties. Mars, a red planet, was always the god of wars, full of energy and aggression. He became the one that got us into trouble. Venus became the planet of love and beauty, the one that gave us sex appeal.

An astrologer will first look at where the planet is placed in a horoscope, in which sign at the moment of birth to tell what influence the planet has on the person's character. If Mars, which indicates a person's drive and assertiveness, is placed in Leo, this indicates a person with a fixed, passionate drive to be a leader. If Mars is in Capricorn, the cardinal earth sign, the drive would be channeled into professional ambition.

Which sign a planet is passing through at the time of an event determines how it will affect the individual's life. Mars passing over a critical point in a horoscope could indicate strife or arguments. It will also show how possible danger or violence can happen at that time.

At first, astrologers only considered the planets that were visible to the naked eye. The sun (really a star), the moon (really a satellite of earth), Mercury, Venus, Mars, Jupiter, and Saturn. Then, in 1781 the planet Uranus was first spotted with a telescope. Neptune was not discovered until 1846 and Pluto as late as 1930. Some astronomers/ astrologers believe that there are even more out there to be found and are already speculating about their personalities.

## The Houses of Your Horoscope: They're Slices of "Life"

The map of the horoscope is drawn like a big round pizza pie, with twelve slices. In the center of the pie, where the slices intersect, is the planet earth, the central point of the horoscope. Each slice is called a house and represents a very specific area of human life. There's a marriage house, a house of career, a house of friends, even a house of the "home." The signs of the zodiac are rotating constantly, as the earth spins on its axis. Therefore, every two hours a sign moves into a new house or "slice of the pizza pie." Since the earth (and the zodiac) rotates completely in twenty-four hours, there are twelve houses.

An astrologer drawing up a horoscope for the moment in time when you were born is going to be very concerned about the exact *place* and *time* you were born. This determines the exact position of the "slice" or house that is on the horizon at that time. For example, 7 p.m. in London, England would be a different part of the house on the horizon than 7 p.m. on the same day in New York because there is a five-hour difference in time.

## The First House Sets up the Horoscope

If your first house has one of the 30 degrees of Aries on a boundary of the slice (called the "cusp" of the house), then Taurus will usually follow on the cusp of the second house, Gemini on the cusp of the third, and so forth. (This is a general rule with many exceptions, because, unike the zodiac, not all houses of the horoscope have an equal size.) This is important to know because, since each house represents an area of human life, the sign on the cusp indictes the personality of the house.

## Your Rising sign Is How You "Face" Life

Your rising sign—or ascendent—is the sign on the cusp of the first house, on the horizon when you were born. If you look at the horoscope pie like the face of a clock the first house would be the 9:40 slice, and the rising sign would be at "9."

As the "leader" of your horoscope, your rising sign shows your special way of presenting yourself to the world. It has to do with your manner, your looks (which is why people may say: "But you don't *look* like a Leo" if you are a Leo with Capricorn rising), and the attitude you project.

The rising sign is the same sign as your sun sign if you were born at sunrise. For instance if you are a Gemini born at sunrise, you would also have

Gemini rising. If you were born two hours later, when the signs change, you would have Cancer rising. Four hours later would give you Leo rising. If you were born later in the day, at sunset, the sign opposite yours on the zodiac wheel, Sagittarius, would be rising.

To find out your rising sign and have a truly accurate horoscope made, you must know the time and place you were born, as exactly as possible. If you don't have this information, an astrologer can do an approximate horoscope, based on what has happened in your life so far. Or a "solar horoscope," where your sun sign is automatically placed on the first house. Most of the general horoscopes in newspapers and magazines are solar horoscopes, where the sun sign is also the rising sign.

The rising sign chart in chapter 13 of this book will give you a reasonable approximation of your rising sign if you know your birthtime within an hour or so.

## Where Your Planets Live Puts Their Houses on the "Map"

Your horoscope, divided up into twelve houses, is populated by ten planets. Some will have a house all to themselves, some will share the house with others ... sometimes several are crowded into one house, depending on how close together they were traveling at the time you were born (or the time of the horoscope being set up). And the more planets you have in a house, the more important that house becomes. It is perfectly possible to have four or more planets jamming up a house, and then that house becomes the focus of the horoscope.

The placement of the planets operates on several levels of meaning. Each planet has its own personality, which is colored by the particular *sign* it is in. Then we have to consider the *house* the planet is in and how it is "decorated" by the sign on the cusp. Is this a conservative Capricorn house with Mars in residence? Mars will be quite at home here, putting his energy to good use. Or a noisy Aries house with sober Saturn at home, putting a damper on the action. Then we consider the house activities. Is it the house that rules marriage, money, work, travel? Which part of life does the house rule and how is it influenced by the sign and the planets inhabiting it.

Now you may be beginning to understand the complicated craft of astrology . . . and why it takes astrologers years to master it. This is not an easy, superficial process, and it takes training and experience to know how to calculate and "weigh" the many different considerations. You may also begin to understand why, with all the variables involved in a horoscope (ten planets, in twelve houses, ruled by twelve signs) no two horoscopes are exactly alike.

**Inter-planetary Relations**

After determining the houses and the location of the planets, the astrologer then looks for the aspects—the ways the planets get along with each other. Some planets will have agreeable aspects to each other: these tend to make life easier for the subject. They could make life "too easy," however. Other planets may have aspects that cramp each other's style: these are going to present challenges in the horoscope.

Technically, an aspect refers to the space between the planets on the 360-degree circle of the horoscope. Some distances are regarded as harmonious . . . the planets help each other out. These are the sextile aspects (planets are 60 degrees apart) or the trine aspects (120 degrees apart). The challenging aspects are the square aspect (90 degrees apart, considered a hard angle) and the opposition (180 degrees) exactly across the zodiac. (Obviously, this last one could mean a tug of war.)

When two or more planets are located within 10 degrees of each other, they are in "conjunction" . . . this is a "double whammy" position where the characters of the planets are thrown together, for better or for worse, depending on the planets involved. The conjunction is always a very powerful aspect in a horoscope. Like a marriage, sometimes the close aspect works, sometimes it doesn't.

Most of us have a combination of challenging and harmonious aspects in our chart. It's one of the things that makes us interesting! How dull if everything were easy in life, nothing would get accomplished and we would never deal with a confrontation or a real challenge. However, too many "hard" angles do not necessarily mean a difficult life. Instead, they could indicate a person who thrives on dealing with confrontations: Used wisely, these could be an asset to a trial lawyer, policeman, or prize fighter. It is how you learn to work with the aspects that can determine the success of your life.

Aspects of the sun will affect your outer life, your basic self, and the energy and courage you will have to make use of life's opportunities.

Aspects of the moon will affect your emotions, your unconscious inner life, what kind of mother a woman will be, and the way a man reacts to women.

Mercury aspects tell how the person thinks, the kind of mind each has, the area of mental interest.

Venus aspects influence how the person will relate closely to others, how well he or she can express love. Mars aspects tell how the native acts—the temperament, outbursts of anger, possible violence.

Jupiter aspects indicate how one cooperates, one's generosity, one's good fortune while Saturn aspects affect discipline, selfishness, rigidity, or flexibility.

Uranus aspects bring on sudden and dramatic changes, originality, or inventiveness. These aspects can show if a person is eccentric or merely unconventional.

Neptune aspects indicate how the person deals with reality, or if there are any transcendental or psychic abilities or a capacity for self-deception. Pluto aspects affect the person's willpower and also how he or she deals with forces beyond their control.

In your relationships with others, how *their* planets aspect *yours* will give you some clues about where problems may arise. Astrologers often do synastry charts (which compare two horoscopes for compatibility) for those clients contemplating marriage or business partnerships. One person's Mars squaring (90 degrees away) another person's Saturn might mean that the Saturn person will frustrate the activity of the Mars person. Other aspects in the two charts might offset this, for example, a moon or Venus trine (60 degrees) Mercury aspect, which indicates good communication.

## The Transiting Planets ... What's Going On Now

Your natal or birth horoscope always remains the same, like a fingerprint. But the planets in the sky will continually change *their* relationships to your natal horoscope throughout your life. The current movements of the planets, particularly when they aspect one of the planets or a sensitive point in your natal horoscope, are called "transits." Transits of Saturn usually mean a period of testing, a Venus transit is when you'll be most attractive to others, a Uranus transit usually means a sudden change. Since the moon changes signs every two days, it is constantly squaring or trining the planets in your chart, which accounts for your emotional "moods." How the transit affects you depends on which planets it involves and which houses these planets are in.

There are several ways to follow the transits each year. An astrologer who knows your horoscope can give you the specific transits which will affect your particular horoscope chart. Or, in the daily forecasts of this book, you can follow the transits of the moon in relationship to your sun sign. The moon passes through all the sun signs each month, aspecting everyone in many ways. You can find the major transits for your sun sign horoscope this year and what they mean in the yearly overview for each sign.

## Planets Make the Road Conditions ... But You're in the Driver's Seat

A horoscope is your guide, your road map, but you must take responsibility for how you use the map. If it's a bumpy road, you go slow. If there's a traffic jam, you watch out; if there is clear sailing, you can breeze ahead with your plans. A specific comparison of your chart and the conditions of the given moment can tell you how you generally react and what is likely to happen. For instance, if Saturn transits a key point such as your rising sign or sun, you will be in for a time of testing. If you know this, you can get in gear to learn from your experiences. A Venus transit of your sun is a time when others will find you most attractive; it's a great time to get out, socialize, or enjoy your romantic life. So you can expect that your horoscope will give you the general conditions. Then it's up to you!

ən. The moon passes through all the sun sign
each month, aspecting everyone in many way

# 3

---

# The Lore and Lure of the Moon

The mysterious moods of the moon are like those of an alluring woman, alternately revealing and then veiling her face in shadows ... keeping a secret side of herself always dark and mysterious, a side she will never reveal to our eyes. The power of the moon pulls at our heartstrings; she inspires us to write love songs or commit crimes of passion. Our moods seem to wax and wane at her whim, one day dreamy, the next day passionate, the next day lighthearted, the next teary. One thing you can say for sure about the mood of the "inconstant" moon is that "this too will pass"—in about two days!

The moon was probably the first heavenly body to prompt us to wonder about the relationship of the heavens to our lives. Why do we feel so "pulled apart" and a bit crazy on the full moon? Why are so many babies born at that time? Why do we feel more energetic on the new moon? Man has pondered these questions since time immemorial and invented legends, lore, and old wives tales to back up his answers.

There are several constant recurring lunar themes. As the sun has always symbolized "male" power and energy, the moon has always been "female" and associated with fertility, growth, and decay. We time the planting and harvesting of crops by the waxing and waning of the moon. Early moon-watchers observed that the moon's cycles closely parallel the fertility cycle in the human female. Thus, in the ancient mythology of many cultures, the moon was personified by goddesses such as Diana or Artemis, who governed reproductive cycles and symbolized both fertility and chastity.

In astrology, the female analogy continues. The moon in a man's chart represents the woman or main female influence in his life. In a woman's horoscope, the moon symbolizes her relationship to powerful female influences, her feminine, receptive side, and the strong martriarchal influence.

The moon's effect on water and its role as reflector, rather than generator, of light prompted its association with our emotions. As we all know, the moon's orbit causes the high and low tides. In astrology, this corresponds to high and low emotional tides. Because the moon reflects both the sun and the vibrations of the zodiac, it takes on different moods, depending on the sign it is transiting.

Each phase, or face, of the moon has its astrological significance in our daily affairs. When the moon is directly opposite the sun in its orbit around the earth, we see it fully illuminated as the full moon. This is the time to bring ideas to fruition, to harvest crops, to go public, to bring matters to a head. It is also the most strongly emotional time, when attractions to the opposite sex are most powerful, when opposing forces confront each other.

When the moon passes close to the sun, it is visible as a mere sliver in the sky. Then, when both the energies of these two luminaries are pulling together is the time to start new projects, to initiate ventures. When the moon is a quarter of the way around its orbit, we see one half of its face illuminated, the other half dark—the "quarter moon." The first quarter after the new moon is good for building on the new project: the last quarter after the full moon is the time for winding down, bringing things to completion, retreating or retrenching.

Occasionally, the sun, moon, and earth are exactly in line and one body will obscure the other—if the moon is completely blocking the sun at the time of the new moon, there will be a solar eclipse. When the earth comes between the sun and moon on a full moon, there is a lunar eclipse. Because these are rare and spectacular occurances, which happen only when the relationship between the axis of the earth and the two heavenly bodies enable an exact lineup, these are very special occasions astrologically. (There will be two lunar eclipses in 1987, on April 13 and October 6.)

When the sun and moon are lined up, as in the new and full moons, the tides are higher (the more direct the line, the higher the tide—so an eclipse will bring an expecially high tide). As the two forces "square" each other on the quarter moon, the tides are lower. This has many analogies in human life. Since our bodies are about 98 percent liquid, we also feel the planetary pull. Blood flows more profusely at the full moon (a bad time for surgery). Emotional disorders are often aggravated because of the pull of the sun and moon from opposite directions ... we seem to be pulled apart (thus the word "lunatic" to describe moon-madness).

The way the moon acts in your life is also influenced by the sign of the zodiac the moon is in at that particular time. It takes about 27 days, 7 hours, and 43 minutes to travel through all the signs, spending about two days in each sign. So the "moods" of the moon change more rapidly than those of any other planet.

Since the full moon is an especially emotional time, the sign each full moon falls in colors it with a special astrological character of its own. Since the sun circles the twelve signs once a year, the full moon will occur in the sign *opposite* the sun. For instance, when the sun is in Scorpio, the full moon will fall in Taurus. Those who will be most affected emotionally will be the zodiac signs which feel the strongest vibrations from the sun and the moon at that time: these are the sun signs, those signs in the "square" aspect, or those whose sun sign is the same sign as the full moon sign. For instance, the above placement (sun in Scorpio, full moon in Taurus) would especially affect the signs of Taurus, Scorpio, Leo, and Aquarius.

Here's a rundown of the full moons for 1987 and what they might mean to you.

**Full Moon in Aries: October 6 (Lunar Eclipse 11:12 p.m.)**     This is a day when the normally cool moon blows "hot." Tempers run high. People are out to get their own way and tend not to listen to reason. The eclipse is going to make this an especially hotheaded time. Aries, Libra, Cancer, and Capricorn are under stress.

**Full Moon in Taurus: November 5**     A very romantic full moon with the sexy Scorpio sun makes people especially ardent. You may tend to "lose" something, however: a personal possession, your heart? Taurus, Scorpio, Aquarius, and Leo are vulnerable.

**Full Moon in Gemini: December 5**     The moon opposite the sun in mutable Sagittarius makes this a hyper day. Stop to think before you act. You could be mentally and emotionally overstimulated. This goes especially for Gemini, Sagittarius, Virgo, and Pisces.

**Full Moon in Cancer: January 14**     This is a watery moon that could bring on the blues or tears. Don't give in to feeling too sorry for yourself. Instead, find comfort by staying home and cuddling with a loved one, especially if you're Cancer, Capricorn, Aries, or Libra.

**Full Moon in Leo: February 13**   Egos are touchy now and ready to explode. So are electrical appliances. Handle everyone with tender loving care today—bring out those velvet gloves. And watch your pocketbook, Aquarius, Leo, Taurus, or Scorpio, you could overspend now.

**Full Moon in Virgo: March 14**   Health matters could come to a head. And all those details you've been postponing could creep up. It's time to do some housecleaning and tidy up in your life, Pisces, Virgo, Sagittarius, and Gemini.

**Full Moon in Libra: April 13 (Eclipse 9.31 p.m.)**   You may be feeling disoriented, off-balance. It is difficult to make decisions or get anything accomplished. It's a much better idea to socialize and meet with friends you really enjoy. This is especially wise for Aries, Libra, Capricorn, and Cancer.

**Full Moon in Scorpio: May 12**   The most crime-prone full moon (also one of the sexiest). Crimes of passion, anger, jealousy, and revenge are on the mind. Keep cool and stay calm at all costs. This goes particularly for Taurus, Scorpio, Aquarius, and Leo.

**Full Moon in Sagittarius: June 11**   Energies are scattered under this mutable moon when people seem to behave irresponsibly. This is a very frustrating moon, better for making plans and looking at the big picture, than carrying them out.

Gemini, Sagittarius, Pisces, and Virgo will be agitated now.

**Full Moon in Capricorn: July 10**   A serious full moon brings financial matters to light; this is the time to pay full attention to serious matters, to older folks, to duties. This goes especially for Capricorn, Cancer, Libra, and Aries.

**Full Moon in Aquarius: August 9**   The Leo sun warms up this cool moon sign with a need to share. This is a time when you'll feel like picking up the check—whether or not you can afford to. Watch the budget, Leo, Aquarius, Taurus, and Scorpio.

**Full Moon in Pisces: September 7**   Watch liquid intake, particularly alcohol. Highly sensitive people tend to drown their sorrows today. Better go to a movie or do something creative and amusing to lift any teary moods. Pay special note to Virgo, Pisces, Gemini, and Sagittarius.

**Moon-Watchers Timetable**

*The New Moon Favors:*
Starting projects
Expending energy
Meeting new people
Planting seeds

*During the First Quarter:*
Build on those projects you've already begun

***The Full Moon Favors:***
Attraction to the opposite sex
Going public
Bringing ideas to fruition
Harvesting crops

***During the Last Quarter:***
Rest and relax
Complete projects
Retrench, review, and analyze your problems

# 4

## The Moon and the Inner You

In your horoscope, the sign of the zodiac where the moon is placed represents your inner receptive emotional nature (the sun is your outer, expressive nature). The moon is what you feel and *need*, what touches you, how things affect you. This can even extend to what foods you like, what colors in your surroundings make you feel good.

The moon rules the "night" of our personality, our subconscious "dark side," which stores our impressions and memories—the basic emotional instincts we remember from childhood—particularly those associated with our mothers and our early nurturing. People with strongly placed moons, such as the moon in the sign of Cancer, which it rules, will be especially influenced by the changes of this planet. Their moods will have more frequent ups and downs, with particular sensitivity at the full moon.

Because the moon is such an important factor

in your horoscope, it is very worthwhile to find your moon. To do this, you must know the time of your birth, as close to the exact hour as possible. Knowing the day and year is not enough: The moon changes signs during the day, approximately every two days. That means you could be born on a day when the moon was in Leo in the morning and then moved into Virgo in the afternoon, giving you the possibility of two completely different emotional natures.

Since the tables which show the changes of the moon are too long to print in this book, you may resort to other methods to find your moon position. One way is to consult a book of tables called an "ephemeris" which charts all the positions of the planets on any given day, going back at least to the turn of the century. These tables are available in most places that sell books on astrology. Another way is to have a computer horoscope done or to have a professional astrologer do your horoscope. A third way is to read through the descriptions of the moon placements of this chapter and see which ones most resemble your own inner feelings. If you do not know the exact time of your birth, you may have to do this anyway (when you read in the ephemeris that there is a change of moon sign on your birthday, read both signs to determine which is most like the inner "you").

# The Lunar Connection in Love

In your romantic relationships, the moon, which governs the needs and emotions is obviously very important. Knowing our partner's moon sign, as well as your own, gives you clues to what your partner "can't live without," to important childhood influences, to what really moves the person, to what will make him or her emotionally happy, to how easily feelings get hurt.

In analyzing a couple's chart for compatibility, astrologers look for a "lunar connection" a harmonious relationship between the moon in one chart and a key planet in the other chart. A sun and moon in a trine or sextile position almost always augurs well for a relationship and can surmount other areas that indicate potential problems.

The good lunar aspects are the moon in the same sign as your loved one's moon sign. This indicates that your emotional natures are similar, even if your sun signs are very diverse. Both your moons in different signs of the same element (fire, earth, air, and water)—if, for example, your lover's moon is in Scorpio and yours is in Cancer— means you will strongly support each other. You will understand each other's feelings without having to work at it. If your moons are in complementary elements (fire with air and earth with water), you will complement each other emotionally, but you will have to make an effort to find out where the other is "coming from."

Some other good lunar connections: your moon in the same sign as your lover's sun or Venus (or vice versa). Again, this indicates an intuitive sympathy, an understanding of what pleases each other, what each other needs, though not necessarily in an emotional way.

Moons in contrasting elements (fire and water, earth and air) make for fascinating chemistry and lots of sexual power. But your emotional instinct will not always be in tune. You won't always be able to sense what the other really needs. And you may have to compromise to make each other happy. How much give and take will be required depends on the relationships between your other planets. If these are harmonious, they may offset any lack of communication here. You will have to *try* harder, in any case.

When your moon is six signs away from your lover's moon, these moons are in opposition. This means they are in complementary elements (earth with water, fire with air), but there is a difference of purpose, a tug in the opposite direction. You may have a lot of emotional confrontations; you may be at cross-purposes from time to time. Again, good communication is necessary; both of you must make an effort and adjust or compromise.

Here is what your moon sign says about your emotional nature:

**Moon in Aries**
This is a fiery moon that does everything passionately . . . or not at all. You demand excitement in your love life. You fall in and out of love too easily. But your enthusiasm and energy can ignite others. You can turn them on, excite them, or

infuriate them. You are naturally independent emotionally and can be quite headstrong and domineering in love. You don't like to be bossed ... ever! You love a challenge and the heat of pursuit, often tiring once the object of your affections is caught ... then it's on to the next! Your emotional life could be long-lasting if you'd learn not to treat your encounters as battles of the sexes, to concentrate on other forms of excitement that you can share with each other.

## Moon in Taurus

Here is a sensualist who feels most amorous when surrounded by beauty and comfort. You need to feel secure in your surroundings, with demonstrations of love and affection. The more trappings—flowers, music, good food, and especially gifts—the better. You are calm, relaxed, and slow to get involved. You are also slow to leave a relationship, once committed. You want to organize a lasting union with lots of physical and material satisfactions. You are stubborn and do not adjust easily—so you are better off finding a partner who will do the compromising or you may have the great fortune to find someone who is completely emotionally compatible, with no effort required on your part.

## Moon in Gemini

Your restless emotional nature could indicate a turbulent love life with lots of highs and lows. You hate to be bored and may agitate your lover deliberately, just to keep things lively. It is especially important to find a lover who stimulates you mentally and creatively. You get satisfaction from public life, rather than home life. You need a constant change of scene—often have more than one home. An active social life with a constantly changing cast of characters is a must. You tend to spread yourself thin emotionally and shy away from deep involvements. You also love to flirt, so you must find a partner who understands your need for outside interests.

## Moon in Cancer

The moon is especially strong in this sign. You need emotional expression—either creatively or professionally and are happiest when you are nurturing others in some way. Some of you are "mothers of the world." This keeps you from indulging in your negative tendency to turn inward and brood. Your home is important to you (many with this placement prefer to work at home or in a homelike atmosphere), and you need a secure, cozy nest. You search for emotional closeness . . . someone who is restful and relaxing and sensitive, who will make you feel emotionally secure.

## Moon in Leo

You're a romanticist who takes everything to heart. You want a love that is on the highest level and often put your beloved on a pedestal. You need to be adored, to receive the total attention of your lover (stay away from flirtatious types). You are also very susceptible to flattery . . . you just love that royal treatment. You are generous with your emotions and your material goods; find someone who enjoys your big heart and won't take advantage of your generosity.

**Moon in Virgo**
You have high standards emotionally and don't give your heart easily. You need to feel that your lover measures up to your ideals. In fairness, you are as critical of yourself as you are of others, and this could keep you from giving your heart at all. You have to learn to accept imperfections in others, to be more demonstrative and sympathetic. You're not a risk-taker and want to feel that everything is neat and tidy emotionally, before you commit yourself.

**Moon in Libra**
This is a moon that is both outgoing and partnership-oriented. You need and value elegance, grace and refinement in all things. You believe in doing things in tandem and love to share all aspects of your life. You are definitely not a loner. But the challenge for you is to find and keep your emotional balance. Not to swing the scales from one extreme to the other. You also need peaceful, harmonious relationships—ones that are light and gay, free and sociable. You hate confrontations and sticky scenes of any kind.

**Moon in Scorpio**
An intense passionate nature goes with this moon. Your feelings run deep and can easily go to extremes. You have strong convictions; you know

what you want. You need emotional and physical closeness and control in your love life. You can also be very possessive. Find an equally passionate person who enjoys and needs to be possessed and stay away from flighty types. You may also channel your emotional need into your work, which could be very healthy for you. Pick a challenging demanding profession like medicine or police work. You're great in life-or-death situations.

## Moon in Sagittarius

Your restless emotional nature may crave exotic adventures in faraway places. Your wanderlust keeps you on the go, and you could have an emotional life that is love 'em and leave 'em. You need an equally independent undemanding partner, whose concept of togetherness includes lots of fun and games . . . and not too much snuggling near the fire. You're not one for staying home at night. A long-distance love affair might be your best bet. You often strive for the unattainable (which keeps you from assuming any responsibility). You need to keep an eye on reality when you set those high goals.

## Moon in Capricorn

You have a strong drive to succeed that will help you surmount obstacles. You'll work hard for and with your partner. But beware of all work and no play. You're a bit of a workaholic and a heavy. Learn to lighten up a bit, have fun. You will find this easier as you grow older. Traditional institutions appeal to you—you are not one for unconventional relationships. You can be devoted to someone who helps you get what and where you want.

## Moon in Aquarius
This is a moon that tends to care more about humanity in general than about a specific person. You need someone who shares your goals and ideals, with whom you have a good intellectual rapport, with whom you can talk about your ideas until late into the night. Leave the emotional heaviness to others ... you prefer a higher level of communication, one that is objective and reasonable. You are experimental and unconventional and could invent your own kind of partnership. You need someone who enjoys your independence, but understands your basic— if unusual—stability. Your emotional nature is unpredictable; you love to surprise and shock others.

## Moon in Pisces
You need and give lots of love and affection, but you are also very sensitive and vulnerable to depression. You need a partner who will get you moving, make you laugh. You tend to cry and feel sorry for yourself. This moon makes you very responsive to whom you are with. You can literally pick up their moods. Therefore it is especially important for you to surround yourself with happy positive influences, soothing and romantic colors, happy people. You need a secure home as a base

for your flights of fantasy and creativity. Your soul mate should bring out your best qualities and talents and respect your sensitivity. Beware of falling for a sob story!

be with... flashes of insight, and... you think. It
will make should bring out your best qualities a...
talents and respect your sensitivity. Beware of l...

# 5

# Your Moon Timing: How to Use the Moon's Day-to-Day Changes

The moon, our closest neighbor in the heavens, is also the heavenly body which moves most quickly around the zodiac. As it orbits the earth, it changes signs—and corresponding vibrations—about every two days. And as it travels, it reflects the special energy and personality each sign brings to our lives.

We are all moved by the power of the moon, just as the moon governs the tides. But the changes will affect us each in different ways as they react with our individual planetary placements. Everytime the moon passes the location of a planet in your horoscope, you will be affected in a certain special way, if only for a few moments, as it races by. For instance, at certain times of the month, when the moon is in a sign favorable to your sun sign, you'll find that life seems to flow more smoothly. At other times you will find it much more difficult to get things done. For instance, in the two days when the moon is traveling through your sun sign, you should feel energized, confident, more powerful. When the moon is in a sign that is in the square aspect (three signs away from your sun sign) or in position (six signs away) you may feel frustrated. By checking out your individual daily forecast in the back of the book, you should be able to schedule your activities to benefit from the most positive "moon days" for you.

Each sign that the moon passes through (and the phase that the moon is in at the time) favors certain activities. Pay attention to the moon sign when you're planning events. To schedule your timetable for success, read on!

## The Moon in Aries
THE MOOD: Quick-tempered, impatient. People are in a hurry to get things done. They may make quick decisions they will later regret. People don't want to stop and think things over. There's a lot of courage and headstrong confidence, but little tact and diplomacy.

*It's a Good Time To:*  Start new projects, do cooking, get a haircut, or sharpen knives; do something spontaneous you've never done before—make an aggressive sales pitch, take an aerobics class, go out for sports.

## The Moon in Taurus
THE MOOD: People are conservative and possessive today. They pull in the reins and keep their eyes on the budget. You'll run into stubbornness,

but appetites for sensual pleasures run high. Better go to a concert and keep away from the refrigerator. You'll crave something sweet and caloric.

*It's a Good Time To:* Make love, sing, tend your garden, buy real estate, or balance your budget, make nonspeculative investments, get a good rest, send flowers, try a gourmet restaurant. Do jobs that require concentration on one thing at a time.

### The Moon in Gemini
THE MOOD: You'll feel a certain restlessness in the air. People are talkative, the phone rings more than usual. It may be difficult to concentrate on any one thing. You may feel a bit scatterbrained and disorganized. People will be feeling sociable, sparkling and witty. Be careful of gossip. It's best to take everything lightly today and stay away from serious projects.

*It's a Good Time To:* Do things that require manual dexterity. You can also do two things at once today. Stick to lightweight projects, however. It's a great day to socialize: Go to a party, write letters, call up old friends, have lunch with friends. You may also feel like pursuing intellectual activities—reading, studying, or signing up for a course. Your language abilities are good now.

### The Moon in Cancer
THE MOOD: Feelings run high today, as people react emotionally to everything. They're sensitive, a bit weepy, and may need mothering. Food and

drink are important now, and people will tend to stay at home hiding in a cozy nest where it's comfortable. People will react emotionally today and tend not to think things through. Family will be especially important now.

*It's a Good Time To:*    Stay home with the family, share a good meal, contact someone from your past, buy antiques, contact your mother, spend time with children, or go for a moonlight walk.

## The Moon in Leo

THE MOOD: It's a show-off day, when you want to look your best, travel first class. You could spend more money than usual. And you could be feeling very romantic. Others may be more bossy and domineering than usual. You search out the sunshine . . . and feel like shining yourself, having some fun and games, going to parties, or perhaps the theater.

*It's a Good Time To:*    Buy clothes, jewelry, cosmetics; get your hair done, show off, dress up, go to elegant places, flirt, treat yourself and others royally, do a creative project, take center stage, make a speech, plan a vacation in the sun, or ask for a loan.

## The Moon in Virgo

THE MOOD: It's time to tidy up and get down to business. Others may be critical today, even nitpicking. People will be holding back money and love. Health gets attention today; check those hypochondriac tendencies. People are very conscious of sloppiness.

*It's a Good Time To:* Stick to your diet, pay attention to your health, buy vitamins, do the crossword puzzle, read, do editing, organize and balance the checkbook, take care of details. But don't ask for a loan today! People will be more tight-fisted than usual.

## The Moon in Libra
THE MOOD: Social, diplomatic, and beauty-loving. Everyone is at his or her most charming. Manners are more genteel. All the rough edges are smoothed down. Everyone is on best behavior and looks swell. People are hoping to share experiences, maybe find a special someone. Romance, in the companionable refined sense, blooms today. It's a time for making the sentimental gesture: Send flowers; open the champagne. Physically beautiful people and surroundings are important today ... any unattractiveness in yourself, your companions or your surroundings will irritate you.

*It's a Good Time To:* Redecorate, beautify yourself, go dancing, learn about the finer things in life, visit an art museum, go to or give a party, have a romantic evening with someone, rest and relax. Not a good day for arguments, aggressive behavior, get up and go.

## The Moon in Scorpio
THE MOOD: This is a sexy moon, with lots of physical passion. People go to extremes of love

and hate. It's a time to watch out for crime—and paranoia—followed by violent rages. The intense energy does help get things done. You'll have the stamina to stick to things. Try to keep temper under control or seek a physical outlet.

*It's a Good time To:* Make love, get to the root of a problem, make a decision, probe your psyche—or that of another person—solve a mystery, keep a secret, get something accomplished or complete a difficult task.

## The Moon in Sagittarius

THE MOOD: It's a light, loose day with plenty of laughs. People are in the mood for outdoor sports, fun and games, gambling, and travel. Everyone tends to think big, has lots of great ideas but may never put them into action. They do make for entertaining get-togethers, though. People are also feeling generous and full of goodwill. They'll take a chance today. Goals are high, but there may be no follow-through.

*It's a Good Time To:* Make a sales pitch, take care of your animals, travel or plan a trip, take care of long-distance business or relatives, pay attention to your spiritual life, take a gamble, tell a joke, mend any fences, get outdoors, and socialize! Forget about saving money, dieting, quiet evenings alone, the budget, and anything else dull and dutiful.

## The Moon in Capricorn

THE MOOD: An about-face from the Sagittarius

moon. Now's the time to pull in your horns and get back to business. You can get a lot done today. Everyone is in a no-nonsense mood . . . and out to use one another. Save the light stuff for another time; this is a serious day. People admire those who project responsibility, self-control, and organization.

*It's a Good Time To:* Plan your investment strategy, visit older relatives, wear your best clothes—the designer labels—buy insurance, organize your life, work overtime, impress the boss.

## The Moon in Aquarius

THE MOOD: People are feeling experimental and interested in trying new things. There's lots of talk about improving the lot of humanity. People are in the mood for gatherings, meetings, politics, community action. They may also feel like throwing over old outworn methods, ideals, and lovers . . . making a drastic change and a new start for the better. It's also a time of surprises and shocks.

*It's a Good Time to:* Join a club or political organization, pay attention to what's happening in the community as a whole, meet with friends, join a discussion group. Change your appearance— maybe a completely new hair color or makeup— tend to electrical gadgets, befriend a stranger, do charity work, do something outrageous, surprise someone.

## The Moon in Pisces

THE MOOD: People are telling and listening to

sob stories; everyone may feel a bit sorry for themselves. Feelings are very tender, easily hurt. You may find it difficult to make decisions—too many emotions getting in the way. It's also easy to misunderstand people; it's better to trust intuition than reason. You will feel more empathetic and your creative projects may get a shot of inspiration. Your loved one will be especially attentive. You may want to fantasize, escape into a dream world, drink too much, have a good cry. Better to go to a movie instead.

*It's a Good Time To:*    Get romantic with someone, tune into your psychic nature, attend a religious service, adopt a pet or a stray person, visit someone in the hospital or in confinement, take photos or movies, go to the movies, work on creative projects, write a poem, go on a crying jag.

# 6

## Venus and Mars . . . What You Want and How You Get It!

In the roster of planets that deal with your relationships to others, each has a role to play. The sun is how you express your *outer nature;* the moon is how you *feel* and what you need to be happy, your inner self. Now comes the planets that show how you woo and win others and what appeals to you most—Venus and Mars.

Venus is known as the planet of love and beauty. In astrology it symbolizes our aesthetic sense, our tastes. It is our sensitivity to refinement, softness, harmony. And it indicates our response to physical beauty. When Venus is in the same sign as your sun sign (once or twice a year), you will be your most attractive self and others will respond favorably to you, especialy the opposite sex.

The position of your Venus when you were born shows how you receive love, how you react, reflecting the character of the sign Venus was passing through at that time. This is a passing planet; it shows what pleases you physically and aesthetically about the outside world.

If you want romance to last in a relationship or you want to attract a special person, it is worthwhile to look up your lover's Venus placement in the chart at the end of this chapter. Your partner's Venus, will show how that individual likes to be made love to—the passive side, what's a turn-on, what you can do to attract and make him or her happy once landed!

Mars is the active doer of the zodiac. It is goal-oriented and shows where you are headed, how you direct your energies, and what you like to do to others. When Mars is passing through your sun sign every two years you will feel your most active and energetic, and your natural drive will be most forceful.

Mars in your horoscope can help you to direct your energies to the place where they will do you the most good. It shows how you actively turn on your partners, how you pursue them; in turn, their Mars will tell you how they will act in return. It will warn you about their red buttons of stress, what makes them angry, when they will take action.

## What to Look for In Your Inter-planetary Relationships

The way the sun, moon, Mars, and Venus interrelate in your own horoscope and between your horoscope and the love interest in your life—or *any* interest, for that matter—can reveal much about how to live with yourself and with others harmoniously.

The easy relationships: when the planets are in the *same sign*, or in the *same element* (fire, earth, air, and water). Or when the planets are in *complementary elements* (fire with air or earth with water).

The challenging relationships: when the planets are in *conflicting elements* (fire or air with earth or water). Or when they are *in opposition*—six signs apart (Aries–Libra, Taurus–Scorpio, Gemini–Sagittarius, Leo–Aquarius, Virgo–Pisces). While you may notice that signs in opposition are in complementary elements, there is always a pull away from each other, from across the zodiac.

**When Venus Aspects the Sun:**
There is a strong mutual support and encouragement if the passive Venus relates well to the active sun. In fact, this is one of the strongest attractions in the zodiac. It is difficult not to be attracted to someone whose Venus is in the same sign as your sun. They flatter you and give you the confidence to express yourself.

A difficult Venus–Sun relationship may result in the active sun person dominating the reactive Venus. Or there may be a fundamental difference in tastes.

**When Venus Aspects the Moon:**
Both of these bodies are reflective and reactive, so this is a peaceful, intuitive relationship, not one that is charged with energy. The giving of emo-

tional security becomes important; there is mutual sensitivity.

Conflicting aspects could mean that the relationship stays on the surface, that the Venus person doesn't really understand the feelings of the moon person; they will irritate each other without knowing why.

## Venus Aspects Mars:
This is the hottest sexual attraction of the zodiac. One partner's Mars aspecting the other's Venus activates it, and this goes even for the "difficult" aspects; sometimes these can be even sexier. In this case, arguments and challenges only stimulate the sex drive more. Smoother aspects will indicate an ability to please the other naturally, without a sexy sparring match to get things going.

## When Venus Aspects Venus:
Easy aspects here show compatible tastes, the same turn-ons. You thoroughly enjoy each other's company—good for harmony and long-lasting friendship. You understand what the other wants and can achieve a balance between these and any other, differing elements in your nature.

## When Mars Aspects the Sun:
These two powerful, active planets can either collide or join forces. Mars in a difficult aspect here can cause much anger and frustration, the will of one person versus the energy of the other. A good aspect means you can *work* well together. There's no clash of egos.

**When Mars Aspects the Moon:**
Mars activates what it touches, so the emotions in this situation will run high. Strong feelings, temper, and sex are energized for better or for worse. If the Mars energy supports the passive emotional moon, all goes well. If not, prepare for stormy weather.

**When Mars Aspects Mars:**
When action meets action, much depends on whether your goals are similar. Can you work in the same direction or will you meet in a head-on collision. Good aspects here mean that your energies complement each other. Difficult aspects could mean you're headed in opposite directions or about to crash.

Look up your Venus and Mars aspects in the chart at the end of this chapter and compare them for some helpful clues on making the best of your relationship.

## Venus and Mars Through the Signs

**Venus in Aries**
You leap headlong into love, preferring a masterful type who sweeps you off your feet. The game of conquest fascinates you more than the possibilities of a relationship, so you're a master of flirting, teasing, all the artful techniques to prolong giving in. You look for constant excitement and stimulation; the quiet life is not for you! You like things loud, hot, and red! Look for a partner who also enjoys love games and lots of action!

## Mars in Aries

Impatience is your middle name. You don't like to wait for anything or anyone. You also must be the boss, and nothing infuriates you more than someone who orders you around. Love is a challenge for you, so you don't mind if there is a little combat first. What happens too easily is no fun. You may find yourself often accused of being selfish or self-centered. If your partner is not in the mood for activities you suggest, you can become disagreeable and sometimes violent. This is the most activist aggressive Mars. You have a hot temper and plenty of energy. You may even pick fights unnecessarily to shake everyone up and create excitement. You must learn to channel some of your competitive energy into healthy outlets via exercise or sports activities.

## Venus in Taurus

This is one of Venus's most sensual positions: you want all of the pleasures of love prolonged as long as possible, please. That means sweet sound and smells, loving touches, delicious tastes, beautiful surroundings and comfort. Not for you, the "quickie" romance. You love to take your time. You fall in love slowly, and it is very difficult for you to leave a relationship once you have settled in. You are a loyal and devoted, if a bit self-indulgent and possessive, partner.

## Mars in Taurus

This is a stubborn Mars position—one with great staying power that doesn't give up easily. The minus side of Mars in Taurus is expressed through a dogmatic, inflexible, tyrannical temperament. You tend to be slow and deliberate, proceeding with a steady pace toward your goals. You are very passionate and giving, also very possessive. You love to own land, beautiful objects—and the one you love. You pursue long-term relationships, not brief affairs, and usually aim for a comfortable one-on-one situation.

## Venus in Gemini

Mental stimulation is a must for this lively Venus. You must have a lover who is interesting. The biggest turn-off is boredom. That's why you often have several lovers at once. (This position is not known for fidelity). The right lover for you must be creative, inventive, always holding back a bit so you can't quite predict the next move. And, because of your roving eye, you should find someone who is equally liberated. A possessive mate will make you want to fly away fast. You love to chatter away, so find a good listener, someone who keeps in constant touch by telephone and enjoys accompanying you on a round of parties and gatherings.

## Mars in Gemini

This mental Mars restlessly pursues variety. You are never quite happy with the way things are. You want a constant change of scenery and lovers. It is very important for you to have an active intellectual and sexual life. You have a very glib tongue and are adept at talking your way into and out of situations. You love to gossip and are known for your witty rejoinders. A problem is your tendency to bore easily; it is difficult for you to stick with anything or anyone for too long. Better go after a nonpossessive partner whose interests are as varied as yours and who gives you lots of space.

## Venus in Cancer

You need to feel secure and emotionally safe before you consider a relationship. This is not a Venus that takes a chance on love. You use your fantastic intuition to detect any false notes and scurry away from danger. You need to feel needed and sometimes can kill a relationship by smothering it. To get through to you, one has to break through your shell of self-protection and calm your fears of getting hurt. Sometimes you will be attracted to someone weaker than you who needs nurturing and protection (you believe there is less possibility of them hurting you). There are many "Sugar Daddies" with this placement. Once committed, however, you hang on for dear life, hating to let go.

## Mars in Cancer

You have a strong nurturing instinct that finds an outlet in your professional or love life. You love to provide food, shelter, and protection for others—and often make your fortune in these areas. You tend to be secretive about your own life, yet cleverly ferret out the secrets of others. You like to make love in familiar, comfortable, homelike surroundings and are one of the zodiac's most tender lovers. You intuitively know what to do and when. To seduce your lover, you use the indirect approach (taking direct action is difficult for many of you), often seeming disinterested while you "sneak up" on the object of your affections. Though you may not like to admit it, you are very ambitious and anxious that the cupboard should never be bare, nor the refrigerator empty. Some of you may be psychologically tied to your family (particularly your mother)—either dependent on relatives or still angry for events which happened in the past.

## Venus in Leo

You want a lover who is also your biggest fan. You can never hear enough flattery, praise, or words of adulation. You should have an appropriate setting for your amours, as you love to go first-class all the way. You also love an elaborate courtship, with all the trimmings ... a beautifully dressed and coifed partner, a fine restaurant or spectacular disco or theatrical event, lots of grand romantic gestures. You also like to receive tokens of affection: candy, flowers, beautiful (and showy) gifts. Look for a lover who takes romance as seriously as you do before you give your heart.

## Mars in Leo

You are a great performer who must live and love wholeheartedly and get much appreciation and applause from those you care for. You tend to make great promises—which you may not be able to deliver—and grand gestures (be sure your credit card is valid before you pick up the check). This is a "big spender" Mars, and nothing is too good for the object of your affections. You go after what you want and love to live life on a grand scale. In a relationship, you are loyal and steady and proud, you love to show off your spouse in regal finery. Angry when put down, you will go to great lengths to top your adversary.

## Venus in Virgo

You could drive your partner crazy by insisting that everything could be a bit more perfect. You have a terrible time deciding what you want—and you often fantasize about the perfect lover, the perfect situation, the perfect setting. It is a key point for you to learn to keep your mouth shut and enjoy! You do love to make sure your partner has all wants and needs satisfied and will go to great lengths to do so, providing that your lover can live up to your own high standards. You could meet this person in a work situation. On the job romance is one of your favorite ways to combine business with pleasure. You could also find romance in a medical or health care situation, you are fascinated with health, exercise, and dietary matters.

## Mars in Virgo

Your standards are often so high that neither you nor anyone else can reach them. So you fantasize a lot, or you try to reform or mold your lovers into your ideal. You are the Pygmalions of the zodiac. You're coolly analytical and very critical—a great asset in business. (No one does the job as well as you.) But in romance, you tend to ignore your partner's need for warmth and feeling. You also may be obessed with cleanliness and sexual technique. It is important for you to learn to express compassion, to become more tolerant and accepting of others' imperfections.

## Venus in Libra

Beauty—in surroundings, in physique, and in compatibility—is your priority. You love the idea of a partnership where you can share everything in perfect harmony and in a beautiful atmosphere, where you can spoil and pamper each other. You also want things to come easily. This is a very lazy Venus, who is attracted to status and luxury. You love beautiful things, giving and receiving gifts on sentimental occasions. (Your lover better remember your birthday.) You also need a decisive partner who can take over and make decisions after you've analyzed the pros and cons.

## Mars in Libra

You are a worshipper of beauty who pursues this in all areas of life. You tend not to make the first move, however. You'll linger indecisively (meanwhile, flirting outrageously), waiting for the other person to pounce or for everything to be perfect. But once inspired, you can create a memorable experience. You aim to do everything artistically, harmoniously, elegantly. You are easily turned off by flaws in your partner or in your surroundings and can seem rather superficial emotionally. But you hate to be alone and search for a partner who can do things in tandem with you. Beware of falling for a flatterer just because you hate to be alone.

## Venus in Scorpio

You're a mystery-lover, attracted to those who don't tell all or show all. You're intense about your relationships; there is no halfway for you. But you are also capable of using your strong sexuality for powerful manipulative purposes. Because you love a challenge, you could be attracted to hard-to-get (and better-off-without) lovers. Then, when you are disapppointed—as is often the case—you are not the type to forgive and forget. You set out for sweet vengeance. You often love extreme types, those with an excess of purity as well as passion. But loyalty is a must; this jealous Venus sends cheaters packing fast.

## Mars in Scorpio

You know what you want and will go to almost any extreme to get it. You are so perceptive that you can automatically assess someone's weak spots— the better to use them for your advantage. You often use your formidable sexual prowess to gain the upper hand. You must always be in control and can withhold love if this gets you where you want to go. When crossed you often extract revenge. This is another Mars position that goes for strategy and games, not an easy conquest. An argument first can get you excited in other ways. You are very jealous, though you may not let on to your partner. A natural detective, you'll ferret out the real story in any situation and retaliate with a mean sting!

## Venus in Sagittarius

This is a love-'em-or-leave-'em Venus that is always on the move. You are fun-loving (with a great sense of humor), a good buddy, and a great romantic. When love goes wrong, you take things philosophically. When it goes right, you'll go places together. You're often attracted to exotic types from faraway places. You prefer love with an idealistic or spiritual partner who can share your ideas and goals. It also helps if they're athletic, with long beautiful legs. You'll want plenty of space in a relationship. If your partner tries to corral you in any way, you'll be out the door in a flash.

## Mars in Sagittarius

You're an adventurer and a romantic wanderer who likes to be fancy-free. Love is a game that requires a philosophical attitude and good sportsmanship all around. It's not to be taken too seriously. Love on the run appeals to you; you are bound to travel much in your lifetime. Your natural good-salesmanship, optimism, and sense of humor win you many easy conquests, which you can leave just as easily and good-naturedly, and you probably leave 'em laughing. You are fun to be with, but you don't stick around for long. You may also promise much more than you deliver. You are direct and devastatingly blunt; you get to the point fast, ignoring tact and diplomacy. And when things get heavy—or someone demands responsibility of you—you're off to the airport.

## Venus in Capricorn
You want a partner who is useful to you and who fits into your scheme of things. No wild eccentrics for you! You're attracted to traditional modes, to marriage, and to fine elegant possessions and surroundings—a fairly conservative image. You may fantasize about one who is just the opposite; however, you'll stick with the tried and true. You may also be attracted to someone with a vastly different age. In any case, you'll improve with age and be a lusty senior citizen.

## Mars in Capricorn
One of the most ambitious positions of Mars. This is a workaholic who loves to be in charge and is intent on climbing socially, politically, and professionally. You'll go after a partner who can elevate your life-style and work alongside you. You'll work at your love life, too, constantly improving your sexual technique. (You may have been a late starter, but you'll get better as you grow older). You are gifted with patience and self-control, plus a keen sense of timing and organization. You may choose older lovers (for power). But you'll stick with someone you can take home to Mama (and secretly have naughty encounters on the sly). You like to plan your sexual encounters beforehand, no rushing in on impulse. You feel responsible, dutiful about sex; your loved one must reach the utmost in pleasure, thanks to your efforts.

## Venus in Aquarius

You tend to steer clear of heavy emotional involvements, preferring someone who engages you mentally, shares your ideals and dedication to finding a worthy cause. For that reason, you can project a rather cool indifferent attitude toward romance. You do love surprises, the unpredictable, the spontaneous. Anything too planned and rigid turns you off. You also like to be and stay friends with your lovers and are great for starting off with a platonic relationship that suddenly becomes *un*platonic. You also love a transcendental experience which takes love out of the ordinary, where there is great "electricity" between you. You could be experimental, even a bit kinky, with your mental approach: The mechanics of the experience can be more exciting than the person. You are often interested in group experiences of all kinds.

## Mars in Aquarius

Because you shy away from deep involvement, you tend to go after "impossible" loves. This means either someone who is already attached, someone unattainable, or someone you have conjured up who exists only in your imagination. You like the surprise experience: A love you can predict will soon bore you, even if it offers security. It is too threatening to your need for independence. You often confuse love and friendship, turning friends into lovers and the reverse. These seem like safe relationships to you, at first, anyway. You love newness—are open to any new ideas, alternate life-styles, and unique domestic arrangements. Since you are not jealous or possessive, you are more likely to invent your own form of loyalty, a unique approach to married life, or you may prefer to stay a loner.

## Venus in Pisces

You love to take care of your lovers and are a real sucker for a sob story. You are also attracted to those who have a physical problem—an ugly duckling, for instance, or someone with an incurable disease—or strays without homes (animals *and* people). You have to be very careful of people taking advantage of you. You are very capable of giving true love and deserve to receive it. You always get emotionally involved and love to give pleasure. You may fall in love too easily and find yourself involved in clandestine affairs and secret meetings. You are also very susceptible to romantic overtures and first-class treatment with a dramatic flair, where you can give vent to your many emotional energies. Avoid playing the martyr and making others feel guilty because of your self-sacrificing nature.

## Mars in Pisces

You tend to scatter your emotional energies in many involvements. You may also play helpless, when you are quite the opposite. This is a great Mars for playing on others' sympathies. You look for lovers to take care of you. It's a great position for actors and actresses, because it enables you to express many emotional natures and gives you great talent for camouflage and illusion. Your energy can be erratic and nerve-racking as you spin a net to ensnare your partner but you can use your sensitivity positively in wonderful soft, sensitive, and caring ways. It is important to find a partner who encourages you to express your talents creatively and provides a strong anchor for your restless emotions.

## VENUS SIGN 1910–1975

| | Aries | Taurus | Gemini | Cancer | Leo | Virgo |
|---|---|---|---|---|---|---|
| **1910** | 5/7-6/3 | 6/4-6/29 | 6/30-7/24 | 7/25-8/18 | 8/19-9/12 | 9/13-10/6 |
| **1911** | 2/28-3/23 | 3/24-4/17 | 4/18-5/12 | 5/13-6/8 | 6/9-7/7 | 7/8-11/8 |
| **1912** | 4/13-5/6 | 5/7-5/31 | 6/1-6/24 | 6/24-7/18 | 7/19-8/12 | 8/13-9/5 |
| **1913** | 2/3-3/6 | 3/7-5/1 | 7/8-8/5 | 8/6-8/31 | 9/1-9/26 | 9/27-10/20 |
| | 5/2-5/30 | 5/31-7/7 | | | | |
| **1914** | 3/14-4/6 | 4/7-5/1 | 5/2-5/25 | 5/26-6/19 | 6/20-7/15 | 7/16-8/10 |
| **1915** | 4/27-5/21 | 5/22-6/15 | 6/16-7/10 | 7/11-8/3 | 8/4-8/28 | 8/29-9/21 |
| **1916** | 2/14-3/9 | 3/10-4/5 | 4/6-5/5 | 5/6-9/8 | 9/9-10/7 | 10/8-11/2 |
| **1917** | 3/29-4/21 | 4/22-5/15 | 5/16-6/9 | 6/10-7/3 | 7/4-7/28 | 7/29-8/21 |
| **1918** | 5/7-6/2 | 6/3-6/28 | 6/29-7/24 | 7/25-8/18 | 8/19-9/11 | 9/12-10/5 |
| **1919** | 2/27-3/22 | 3/23-4/16 | 4/17-5/12 | 5/13-6/7 | 6/8-7/7 | 7/8-11/8 |
| **1920** | 4/12-5/6 | 5/7-5/30 | 5/31-6/23 | 6/24-7/18 | 7/19-8/11 | 8/12-9/4 |
| **1921** | 2/3-3/6 | 3/7-4/25 | 7/8-8/5 | 8/6-8/31 | 9/1-9/25 | 9/26-10/20 |
| | 4/26-6/1 | 6/2-7/7 | | | | |
| **1922** | 3/13-4/6 | 4/7-4/30 | 5/1-5/25 | 5/26-6/19 | 6/20-7/14 | 7/15-8/9 |
| **1923** | 4/27-5/21 | 5/22-6/14 | 6/15-7/9 | 7/10-8/3 | 8/4-8/27 | 8/28-9/20 |
| **1924** | 2/13-3/8 | 3/9-4/4 | 4/5-5/5 | 5/6-9/8 | 9/9-10/7 | 10/8-11/12 |
| **1925** | 3/28-4/20 | 4/21-5/15 | 5/16-6/8 | 6/9-7/3 | 7/4-7/27 | 7/28-8/21 |
| **1926** | 5/7-6/2 | 6/3-6/28 | 6/29-7/23 | 7/24-8/17 | 8/18-9/11 | 9/12-10/5 |
| **1927** | 2/27-3/22 | 3/23-4/16 | 4/17-5/11 | 5/12-6/7 | 6/8-7/7 | 7/8-11/9 |
| **1928** | 4/12-5/5 | 5/6-5/29 | 5/30-6/23 | 6/24-7/17 | 7/18-8/11 | 8/12-9/4 |
| **1929** | 2/3-3/7 | 3/8-4/19 | 7/8-8/4 | 8/5-8/30 | 8/31-9/25 | 9/26-10/19 |
| | 4/20-6/2 | 6/3-7/7 | | | | |
| **1930** | 3/13-4/5 | 4/6-4/30 | 5/1-5/24 | 5/25-6/18 | 6/19-7/14 | 7/15-8/9 |
| **1931** | 4/26-5/20 | 5/21-6/13 | 6/14-7/8 | 7/9-8/2 | 8/3-8/26 | 8/27-9/19 |

| Libra | Scorpio | Sagittarius | Capricorn | Aquarius | Pisces |
|---|---|---|---|---|---|
| 10/7-10/30 | 10/31-11/23 | 11/24-12/17 | 12/18-12/31 | 1/1-1/15 | 1/16-1/28 |
| | | | | 1/29-4/4 | 4/5-5/6 |
| 11/19-12/8 | 12/9-12/31 | | 1/1-1/10 | 1/11-2/2 | 2/3-2/27 |
| 9/6-9/30 | 1/1-1/4 | 1/5-1/29 | 1/30-2/23 | 2/24-3/18 | 3/19-4/12 |
| | 10/1-10/24 | 10/25-11/17 | 11/18-12/12 | 12/13-12/31 | |
| 10/21-11/13 | 11/14-12/7 | 12/8-12/31 | | 1/1-1/6 | 1/7-2/2 |
| | | | | | |
| 8/11-9/6 | 9/7-10/9 | 10/10-12/5 | 1/1-1/24 | 1/25-2/17 | 2/18-3/13 |
| | 12-6/12-30 | 12/31 | | | |
| 9/22-10/15 | 10/16-11/8 | 1/1-1/26 | 2/7-3/6 | 3/7-4/1 | 4/2-4/26 |
| | | 11/9-12/2 | 12/3-12/26 | 12/27-12/31 | |
| 11/3-11/27 | 11/28-12/21 | 12/22-12/31 | | 1/1-1/19 | 1/20-2/13 |
| 8/22-9/16 | 9/17-10/11 | 1/1-1/14 | 1/15-2/7 | 2/8-3/4 | 3/5-3/28 |
| | | 10/12-11/6 | 11/7-12/5 | 12/6-12/31 | |
| 10/6-10/29 | 10/30-11/22 | 11/23-12/16 | 12/17-12/31 | 1/1-4/5 | 4/6-5/6 |
| 11/9-12/8 | 12/9-12/31 | | 1/1-1/9 | 1/10-2/2 | 2/3-2/26 |
| 9/5-9/30 | 1/1-1/3 | 1/4-1/28 | 1/29-2/22 | 2/23-3/18 | 3/19-4/11 |
| | 9/31-10/23 | 10/24-11/17 | 11/18-12/11 | 12/12-12/31 | |
| 10/21-11/13 | 11/14-12/7 | 12/8-12/31 | | 1/1-1/6 | 1/7-2/2 |
| 8/10-9/6 | 9/7-10/10 | 10/11-11/28 | 1/1-1/24 | 1/25-2/16 | 2/17-3/12 |
| | 11/29-12/31 | | | | |
| 9/21-10/14 | 1/1 | 1/2-2/6 | 2/7-3/5 | 3/6-3/31 | 4/1-4/26 |
| | 10/15-11/7 | 11/8-12/1 | 12/2-12/25 | 12/26-12/31 | |
| 11/3-11/26 | 11/27-12/21 | 12/22-12/31 | | 1/1-1/19 | 1/20-2/12 |
| 8/22-9/15 | 9/16-10/11 | 1/1-1/14 | 1/15-2/7 | 2/8-3/3 | 3/4-3/27 |
| | | 10-12/11-6 | 11/7-12/5 | 12/6-12/31 | |
| 10/6-10/29 | 10/30-11/22 | 11/23-12/16 | 12/17-12/31 | 1/1-4/5 | 4/6-5/6 |
| 11/10-12/8 | 12/9-12/31 | 1/1-1/7 | 1/8 | 1/9-2/1 | 2/2-2/26 |
| 9/5-9/28 | 1/1-1/3 | 1/4-1/28 | 1/29-2/22 | 2/23-3/17 | 3/18-4/11 |
| | 9/29-10/23 | 10/24-11/16 | 11/17-12/11 | 12/12-12/31 | |
| 10/20-11/12 | 11/13-12/6 | 12/7-12/30 | 12/31 | 1/1-1/5 | 1/6-2/2 |
| | | | | | |
| 8/10-9/6 | 9/7-10/11 | 10/12-11/21 | 1/1-1/23 | 1/24-2/16 | 2/17-3/12 |
| | 11/22-12/31 | | | | |
| 9/20-10/13 | 1/1-1/3 | 1/4-2/6 | 2/7-3/4 | 3/5-3/31 | 4/1-4/25 |
| | 10/14-11/6 | 11/7-11/30 | 12/1-12/24 | 12/25-12/31 | |

|      | Aries      | Taurus     | Gemini     | Cancer     | Leo         | Virgo       |
|------|------------|------------|------------|------------|-------------|-------------|
| 1932 | 2/12-3/8   | 3/9-4/3    | 4/4-5/5    | 5/6-7/12   | 9/9-10/6    | 10/7-11/1   |
|      |            |            | 7/13-7/27  | 7/28-9/8   |             |             |
| 1933 | 3/27-4/19  | 4/20-5/28  | 5/29-6/8   | 6/9-7/2    | 7/3-7/26    | 7/27-8/20   |
| 1934 | 5/6-6/1    | 6/2-6/27   | 6/28-7/22  | 7/23-8/16  | 8/17-9/10   | 9/11-10/4   |
| 1935 | 2/26-3/21  | 3/22-4/15  | 4/16-5/10  | 5/11-6/6   | 6/7-7/6     | 7/7-11/8    |
| 1936 | 4/11-5/4   | 5/5-5/28   | 5/29-6/22  | 6/23-7/16  | 7/17-8/10   | 8/11-9/4    |
| 1937 | 2/2-3/8    | 3/9-4/17   | 7/7-8/3    | 8/4-8/29   | 8/30-9/24   | 9/25-10/18  |
|      | 4/14-6/3   | 6/4-7/6    |            |            |             |             |
| 1938 | 3/12-4/4   | 4/5-4/28   | 4/29-5/23  | 5/24-6/18  | 6/19-7/13   | 7/14-8/8    |
| 1939 | 4-25/5/19  | 5/20-6/13  | 6/14-7/8   | 7/9-8/1    | 8/2-8/25    | 8/26-9/19   |
| 1940 | 2/12-3/7   | 3/8-4/3    | 4/4-5/5    | 5/6-7/4    | 9/9-10/5    | 10/6-10/31  |
|      |            |            | 7/5-7/31   | 8/1-9/8    |             |             |
| 1941 | 3/27-4/19  | 4/20-5/13  | 5/14-6/6   | 6/7-6/1    | 7/2-7/26    | 7/27-8/20   |
| 1942 | 5/6-6/1    | 6/2-6/26   | 6/27-7/22  | 7/23-8/16  | 8/17-9/9    | 9/10-10/3   |
| 1943 | 2/25-3/20  | 3/21-4/14  | 4/15-5/10  | 5/11-6/6   | 6/7-7/6     | 7/7-11/8    |
| 1944 | 4-10/5-3   | 5/4-5/28   | 5/29-6/21  | 6/22-7/16  | 7/17-8/9    | 8/10-9/2    |
| 1945 | 2/2-3/10   | 3/11-4/6   | 7/7-8/3    | 8/4-8/29   | 8/30-9/23   | 9/24-10/18  |
|      | 4/7-6/3    | 6/4-7/6    |            |            |             |             |
| 1946 | 3/11-4/4   | 4/5-4/28   | 4/29-5/23  | 5/24-6/17  | 6/18-7/12   | 7/13-8/8    |
| 1947 | 4/25-5/19  | 5/20-6/12  | 6/13-7/7   | 7/8-8/1    | 8/2-8/25    | 8/26-9/18   |
| 1948 | 2/11-3/7   | 3/8-4/3    | 4/4-5/6    | 5/7-6/28   | 9/8-10/5    | 10/6-10/31  |
|      |            |            | 6/29-8/2   | 8/3-9/7    |             |             |
| 1949 | 3/26-4/19  | 4/20-5/13  | 5/14-6/6   | 6/7-6/30   | 7/1-7/25    | 7/26-8/19   |
| 1950 | 5/5-5/31   | 6/1-6/26   | 6/27-7/21  | 7/22-8/15  | 8/16-9/9    | 9/10-10/3   |
| 1951 | 2/25-3/21  | 3/22-4/15  | 4/16-5/10  | 5/11-6/6   | 6/7-7/7     | 7/8-11/9    |
| 1952 | 4/10-5/4   | 5/5-5/28   | 5/29-6/21  | 6/22-7/16  | 7/17-8/9    | 8/10-9/3    |
| 1953 | 2/2-3/13   | 3/4-3/31   | 7/8-8/3    | 8/4-8/29   | 8/30-9/24   | 9/25-10/18  |
|      | 4/1-6/5    | 6/6-7/7    |            |            |             |             |

## VENUS SIGN 1910–1975

| Libra | Scorpio | Sagittarius | Capricorn | Aquarius | Pisces |
|---|---|---|---|---|---|
| 11/2-11/25 | 11/26-12/20 | 12/21-12/31 | | 1/1-1/18 | 1/19-2/11 |
| | | | | | |
| 8/21-9/14 | 9/15-10/10 | 1/1-1/13 | 1/14-2/6 | 2/7-3/2 | 3/3-3/26 |
| | | 10/11-11/5 | 11/6-12/4 | 12/5-12/31 | |
| 10/5-10/28 | 10/29-11/21 | 11/22-12/15 | 12/16-12/31 | 1/1-4/5 | 4/6-5/5 |
| 11/9-12/7 | 12/8-12/31 | | 1/1-1/7 | 1/8-1/31 | 2/1-2/25 |
| 9/5-9/27 | 1/1-1/2 | 1/3-1/27 | 1/28-2/21 | 2/22-3/16 | 3/17-4/10 |
| | 9/28-10/22 | 10/23-11/15 | 11/16-12/10 | 12/11-12/31 | |
| 10/19-11/11 | 11/12-12/5 | 12/6-12/29 | 12/30-12/31 | 1/1-1/5 | 1/6-2/1 |
| | | | | | |
| 8/9-9/6 | 9/7-10/13 | 10/14-11/14 | 1/1-1/22 | 1/23-2/15 | 2/16-3/11 |
| | 11/15-12/31 | | | | |
| 9/20-10/13 | 1/1-1/3 | 1/4-2/5 | 2/6-3/4 | 3/5-3/30 | 3/31-4/24 |
| | 10/14-11/6 | 11/7-11/30 | 12/1-12/24 | 12/25-12/31 | |
| 11/1-11/25 | 11/26-12/19 | 12/20-12/31 | | 1/1-1/18 | 1/19-2/11 |
| | | | | | |
| 8/21-9/14 | 9/15-10/9 | 1/1-1/12 | 1/13-2/5 | 2/6-3/1 | 3/2-3/26 |
| | | 10/10-11/5 | 11/6-12/4 | 12/5-12/31 | |
| 10/4-10/27 | 10/28-11/20 | 11/21-12/14 | 12/15-12/31 | 1/1-4/4 | 4/6-5/5 |
| 11/9-12/7 | 12/8-12/31 | | 1/1-1/7 | 1/8-1/31 | 2/1-2/24 |
| 9/3-9/27 | 1/1-1/2 | 1/3-1/27 | 1/28-2/20 | 2/21-3/16 | 3/17-4/9 |
| | 9/28-10/21 | 10/22-11/15 | 11/16-12/10 | 12/11-12/31 | |
| 10/19-11/11 | 11/12-12/5 | 12/6-12/29 | 12/30-12/31 | 1/1-1/4 | 1/5-2/1 |
| | | | | | |
| 8/9-9/6 | 9/7-10/15 | 10/16-11/7 | 1/1-1/21 | 1/22-2/14 | 2/15-3/10 |
| | 11/8-12/31 | | | | |
| 9/19-10/12 | 1/1-1/4 | 1/5-2/5 | 2/6-3/4 | 3/5-3/29 | 3/30-4/24 |
| | 10/13-11/5 | 11/6-11/29 | 11/30-12/23 | 12/24-12/31 | |
| 11/1-1/25 | 11/26-12/19 | 12/20-12/31 | | 1/1-1/17 | 1/18-2/10 |
| | | | | | |
| 8/20-9/14 | 9/15-10/9 | 1/1-1/12 | 1/13-2/5 | 2/6-3/1 | 3/2-3/25 |
| | | 10/10-11/5 | 11/6-12/5 | 12/6-12/31 | |
| 10/4-10/27 | 10/28-11/20 | 11/21-12/13 | 12/14-12/31 | 1/1-4/5 | 4/6-5/4 |
| 11/10-12/7 | 12/8-12/31 | | 1/1-1/7 | 1/8-1/31 | 2/1-2/24 |
| 9/4-9/27 | 1/1-1/2 | 1/3-1/27 | 1/28-2/20 | 2/21-3/16 | 3/17-4/9 |
| | 9/28-10/21 | 10/22-11/15 | 11/16-12/10 | 12/11-12/31 | |
| 10/19-11/11 | 11/12-12/5 | 12/6-12/29 | 12/30-12/31 | 1/1-1/5 | 1/6-2/1 |

## VENUS SIGN 1910–1975

| | Aries | Taurus | Gemini | Cancer | Leo | Virgo |
|---|---|---|---|---|---|---|
| 1954 | 3/12-4/4 | 4/5-4/28 | 4/29-5/23 | 5/24-6/17 | 6/18-7/13 | 7/14-8/8 |
| 1955 | 4/25-5/19 | 5/20-6/13 | 6/14-7/7 | 7/8-8/1 | 8/2-8/25 | 8/26-9/18 |
| 1956 | 2/12-3/7 | 3/8-4/4 | 4/5-5/7 6:24-8/4 | 5/8-6/23 8/5-9/8 | 9/9-10/5 | 10/6-10/31 |
| 1957 | 3-26/4-19 | 4/20-5/13 | 5/14-6/6 | 6/7-7/1 | 7/2-7/26 | 7/27-8/19 |
| 1958 | 5-6/5-31 | 6/1-6/26 | 6/27-7/22 | 7/23-8/15 | 8/16-9/9 | 9/10-10/3 |
| 1959 | 2-25/3-20 | 3/21-4/14 | 4/15-5/10 | 5/11-6/6 | 6/7-7/8 9/21-9/24 | 7/9-9/20 9/25-11/9 |
| 1960 | 4-10/5-3 | 5/4-5/28 | 5/29-6/21 | 6/22-7/15 | 7/16-8/9 | 8/10-9/2 |
| 1961 | 2-3/6-5 | 6/6-7/7 | 7/8-8/3 | 8/4-8/29 | 8/30-9/23 | 9/24-10/17 |
| 1962 | 3/11-4/3 | 4/4-4/28 | 4/29-5/22 | 5/23-6/17 | 6/18-7/12 | 7/13-8/8 |
| 1963 | 4/24-5/18 | 5/19-6/12 | 6/13-7/7 | 7/8-7/31 | 8/1-8/25 | 8/26-9/18 |
| 1964 | 2/11-3/7 | 3/8-4/4 | 4/5-5/9 6/18-8/5 | 5/10-6/17 8/6-9/8 | 9/9-10/5 | 10/6-10/31 |
| 1965 | 3/26-4/18 | 4/19-5/12 | 5/13-6/6 | 6/7-6/30 | 7/1-7/25 | 7/26-8/19 |
| 1966 | 5/6-6/31 | 6/1-6/26 | 6/27-7/21 | 7/22-8/15 | 8/16-9/8 | 9/9-10/2 |
| 1967 | 2/24-3/20 | 3/21-4/14 | 4/15-5/10 | 5/11-6/6 | 6/7-7/8 9/10-10/1 | 7/9-9/9 10/2-11/9 |
| 1968 | 4/9-5/3 | 5/4-5/27 | 5/28-6/20 | 6/21-7/15 | 7/16-8/8 | 8/9-9/2 |
| 1969 | 2/3-6/6 | 6/7-7/6 | 7/7-8/3 | 8/4-8/28 | 8/29-9/22 | 9/23-10/17 |
| 1970 | 3/11-4/3 | 4/4-4/27 | 4/28-5/22 | 5/23-6/16 | 6/17-7/12 | 7/13-8/8 |
| 1971 | 4/24-5/18 | 5/19-6/12 | 6/13-7/6 | 7/7-7/31 | 8/1-8/24 | 8/25-9/17 |
| 1972 | 2/11-3/7 | 3/8-4/3 | 4/4-5/10 6/12-8/6 | 5/11-6/11 8/7-9/8 | 9/9-10/5 | 10/6-10/30 |
| 1973 | 3/25-4/18 | 4/18-5/12 | 5/13-6/5 | 6/6-6/29 | 7/1-7/25 | 7/26-8/19 |
| 1974 | | | | | | |
| | 5/5-5/31 | 6/1-6/25 | 6/26-7/21 | 7/22-8/14 | 8/15-9/8 | 9/9-10/2 |
| 1975 | 2/24-3/20 | 3/21-4/13 | 4/14-5/9 | 5/10-6/6 | 6/7-7/9 9/3-10/4 | 7/10-9/2 10/5-11/9 |

# VENUS SIGN 1910–1975

| Libra | Scorpio | Sagittarius | Capricorn | Aquarius | Pisces |
|---|---|---|---|---|---|
| 8/9-9/6 | 9/7-10/22 | 10/23-10/27 | 1/1-1/22 | 1/23-2/15 | 2/16-3/11 |
| | 10/28-12/31 | | | | |
| 9/19-10/13 | 1/1-1/6 | 1/7-2/5 | 2/6-3/4 | 3/5-3/30 | 3/31-4/24 |
| | 10/14-11/5 | 11/6-11/30 | 12/1-12/24 | 12/25-12/31 | |
| 11/1-11/25 | 11/26-12/19 | 12/20-12/31 | | 1/1-1/17 | 1/18-2/11 |
| | | | | | |
| 8/20-9/14 | 9/15-10/9 | 1/1-1/12 | 1/13-2/5 | 2/6-3/1 | 3/2-3/25 |
| | | 10/10-11/5 | 11/6-12/16 | 12/7-12/31 | |
| 10/4-10/27 | 10/28-11/20 | 11/21-12/14 | 12/15-12/31 | 1/1-4/6 | 4/7-5/5 |
| 11/10-12/7 | 12/8-12/31 | | 1/1-1/7 | 1/8-1/31 | 2/1-2/24 |
| | | | | | |
| 9/3-9/26 | 1/1-1/2 | 1/3-1/27 | 1/28-2/20 | 2/21-3/15 | 3/16-4/9 |
| | 9/27-10/21 | 10/22-11/15 | 11/16-12/10 | 12/11-12/31 | |
| 10/18-11/11 | 11/12-12/4 | 12/5-12/28 | 12/29-12/31 | 1/1-1/5 | 1/6-2/2 |
| 8/9-9/6 | 9/7-12/31 | | 1/1-1/21 | 1/22-2/14 | 2/15-3/10 |
| 9/19-10/12 | 1/1-1/6 | 1/7-2/5 | 2/6-3/4 | 3/5-3/29 | 3/30-4/23 |
| | 10/13-11/5 | 11/6-11/29 | 11/30-12/23 | 12/24-12/31 | |
| 11/1-11/24 | 11/25-12/19 | 12/20-12/31 | | 1/1-1/16 | 1/17-2/10 |
| | | | | | |
| 8/20-9/13 | 9/14-10/9 | 1/1-1/12 | 1/13-2/5 | 2/6-3/1 | 3/2-3/25 |
| | | 10/10-11/5 | 11/6-12/7 | 12/8-12/31 | |
| 10/3-10/26 | 10/27-11/19 | 11/20-12/13 | 2/7-2/25 | 1/1-2/6 | 4/7-5/5 |
| | | | 12/14-12/31 | 2/26-4/6 | |
| 11/10-12/7 | 12/8-12/23 | | 1/1-1/6 | 1/7-1/30 | 1/31-2/23 |
| | | | | | |
| 9/3-9/26 | 1/1 | 1/2-1/26 | 1/27-2/20 | 2/21-3/15 | 3/16-4/8 |
| | 9/27-10/21 | 10/22-11/14 | 11/15-12/9 | 12/10-12/31 | |
| 10/18-11/10 | 11/11-12/4 | 12/5-12/28 | 12/29-12/31 | 1/1-1/4 | 1/5-2/2 |
| 8/9-9/7 | 9/8-12/31 | | 1/1-1/21 | 1/22-2/14 | 2/15-3/10 |
| 9/18-10/11 | 1/1-1/7 | 1/8-2/5 | 2/6-3/4 | 3/5-3/29 | 3/30-4/23 |
| | 10/12-11/5 | 11/6-11/29 | 11/30-12/23 | 12/24-12/31 | |
| | 11/25-12/18 | 12/19-12/31 | | 1/1-1/16 | 1/17-2/10 |
| 10/31-11/24 | | | | | |
| 8/20-9/13 | | 1/1-1/12 | 1/13-2/4 | 2/5-2/28 | 3/1-3/24 |
| | | 10/9-11/5 | 11/6-12/7 | 12/8-12/31 | |
| | | | 1/30-2/28 | 1/1-1/29 | |
| 10/3-10/26 | 10/27-11/19 | 11/20-12/13 | 12/14-12/31 | 3/1-4/6 | 4/7-5/4 |
| | | | 1/1-1/6 | 1/7-1/30 | 1/31-2/23 |
| 11/10-12/7 | 12/8-12/31 | | | | |

| | Jan. | Feb. | Mar. | Apr. | May | June | July | Aug. | Sept. | Oct. | Nov. | Dec. |
|---|---|---|---|---|---|---|---|---|---|---|---|---|
| 1910 | AR | TA | GE | GE | CA | CA | LE | VI | VI | LI | SC | SC |
| 1911 | SA | CP | AQ | AQ | PI | AR | TA | TA | GE | GE | GE | TA |
| 1912 | TA | GE | GE | CA | CA | LE | LE | VI | LI | LI | SC | SA |
| 1913 | CP | CP | AQ | PI | AR | AR | TA | GE | CA | CA | CA | CA |
| 1914 | CA | CA | CA | CA | LE | LE | VI | LI | LI | SC | SA | SA |
| 1915 | CP | AQ | PI | PI | AR | TA | GE | GE | CA | LE | LE | LE |
| 1916 | LE | LE | LE | LE | LE | VI | VI | LI | SC | SC | SA | CP |
| 1917 | AQ | AQ | PI | AR | TA | GE | GE | CA | LE | LE | VI | VI |
| 1918 | LI | LI | VI | VI | VI | VI | LI | LI | SC | SA | CP | CP |
| 1919 | AQ | PI | AR | TA | GE | CA | CA | LE | VI | VI | VI | LI |
| 1920 | LI | SC | SC | SC | LI | LI | SC | SC | SA | SA | CP | AQ |
| 1921 | PI | AR | AR | TA | GE | GE | CA | LE | LE | VI | LI | LI |
| 1922 | SC | SC | SA | SA | SA | SA | SC | SA | CP | CP | AQ | AQ |
| 1923 | PI | AR | TA | TA | GE | CA | CA | LE | VI | VI | LI | SC |
| 1924 | SC | SA | CP | CP | AQ | AQ | PI | PI | AQ | AQ | PI | PI |
| 1925 | AR | TA | TA | GE | CA | CA | LE | VI | VI | LI | SC | SC |
| 1926 | SA | CP | CP | AQ | PI | AR | AR | TA | TA | TA | TA | TA |
| 1927 | TA | TA | GE | GE | CA | LE | LE | VI | LI | LI | SC | SA |
| 1928 | SA | SA | AQ | PI | PI | AR | TA | GE | GE | CA | CA | CA |

92

## MARS SIGN 1910–1975

| | Jan. | Feb. | Mar. | Apr. | May | June | July | Aug. | Sept. | Oct. | Nov. | Dec. |
|------|------|------|------|------|------|------|------|------|-------|------|------|------|
| 1929 | GE | GE | CA | CA | LE | LE | VI | VI | LI | SC | SC | SA |
| 1930 | CP | AQ | AQ | PI | AR | TA | GE | GE | CA | CA | LE | LE |
| 1931 | LE | LE | CA | LE | LE | VI | VI | LI | LI | SC | SA | CP |
| 1932 | CP | AQ | PI | AR | TA | TA | GE | CA | CA | LE | VI | VI |
| 1933 | VI | VI | VI | VI | VI | VI | LI | LI | LI | SA | SA | CP |
| 1934 | AQ | PI | AR | AR | TA | GE | GE | CA | LE | LE | VI | LI |
| 1935 | LI | LI | LI | LI | LI | LI | LI | SC | SC | SA | CP | LI |
| 1936 | PI | PI | AR | TA | GE | GE | CA | LE | LE | VI | LI | AQ |
| 1937 | SC | SC | SA | SA | SC | SC | SC | SA | SA | CP | AQ | AQ |
| 1938 | PI | AR | TA | TA | GE | CA | CA | LE | VI | VI | LI | SC |
| 1939 | SC | SA | SA | CP | CP | AQ | AQ | CP | CP | AQ | AQ | PI |
| 1940 | AR | SA | TA | CP | GE | CA | LE | LE | VI | VI | LI | SC |
| 1941 | SA | TA | CP | GE | AQ | PI | AR | AR | AR | AR | AR | AR |
| 1942 | TA | CP | GE | AQ | CA | LE | LE | VI | VI | LI | SC | SC |
| 1943 | SA | GE | AQ | GE | PI | AR | TA | TA | GE | GE | GE | GE |
| 1944 | GE | GE | GE | AQ | CA | LE | VI | VI | LI | SC | SC | SA |
| 1945 | CP | AQ | AQ | PI | AR | TA | TA | GE | CA | SC | LE | LE |
| 1946 | CA | CA | AQ | CA | LE | LE | VI | LI | LI | SC | SA | SA |
| 1947 | CP | AQ | PI | AR | AR | TA | GE | CA | CA | LE | LE | VI |

| | Jan. | Feb. | Mar. | Apr. | May | June | July | Aug. | Sept. | Oct. | Nov. | Dec. |
|---|---|---|---|---|---|---|---|---|---|---|---|---|
| 1948 | VI | LE | LE | LE | LE | VI | VI | LI | SC | SC | SA | CP |
| 1949 | AQ | PI | PI | AR | TA | GE | GE | CA | LE | LE | VI | VI |
| 1950 | LI | LI | LI | VI | VI | LI | LI | SC | SC. | SA | CP | CP |
| 1951 | AQ | PI | AR | TA | TA | GE | CA | CA | LE | VI | VI | LI |
| 1952 | LI | SC | SC | SC | SC | SC | SC | SC | SA | CP | CP | AQ |
| 1953 | AR | AR | AR | TA | GE | GE | CA | LE | VI | VI | LI | LI |
| 1954 | SC | SA | SA | CP | CP | CP | SA | SA | CP | CP | AQ | PI |
| 1955 | PI | AR | TA | GE | GE | CA | LE | LE | VI | LI | LI | SC |
| 1956 | SA | SA | CP | AQ | AQ | PI | PI | PI | PI | PI | PI | AR |
| 1957 | AR | TA | TA | GE | CA | CA | LE | VI | VI | LI | SC | SC |
| 1958 | SA | CP | CP | AQ | PI | AR | AR | TA | TA | GE | TA | TA |
| 1959 | TA | GE | GE | CA | CA | LE | LE | VI | LI | LI | SC | SA |
| 1960 | CP | CP | AQ | PI | AR | AR | TA | GE | GE | CA | CA | CA |
| 1961 | CA | CA | CA | CA | LE | LE | VI | VI | LI | SC | SA | SA |
| 1962 | CP | AQ | PI | PI | AR | TA | GE | GE | CA | LE | LE | LE |
| 1963 | LE | LE | LE | LE | LE | VI | VI | LI | SC | LE | SA | CP |
| 1964 | AQ | AQ | PI | AR | TA | TA | GE | CA | LE | SC | VI | VI |
| 1965 | VI | VI | VI | VI | VI | VI | LI | LI | SC | SA | CP | CP |
| 1966 | AQ | PI | AR | AR | TA | GE | CA | CA | LE | VI | VI | LI |

## MARS SIGN 1910–1975

| | Jan. | Feb. | Mar. | Apr. | May | June | July | Aug. | Sept. | Oct. | Nov. | Dec. |
|---|---|---|---|---|---|---|---|---|---|---|---|---|
| 1967 | LI | SC | SC | LI | LI | LI | LI | SC | SA | SA | CP | AQ |
| 1968 | PI | PI | AR | TA | GE | GE | CA | LE | LE | VI | LI | LI |
| 1969 | SC | SC | SA | SA | SA | SA | SA | SA | SA | CP | AQ | PI |
| 1970 | PI | AR | TA | TA | GE | CA | CA | LE | VI | VI | LI | SC |
| 1971 | SC | SA | CP | CP | AQ | AQ | AQ | AQ | AQ | AQ | PI | PI |
| 1972 | AR | TA | TA | GE | CA | CA | LE | LE | VI | LI | SC | SC |
| 1973 | SA | CP | CP | AQ | PI | PI | AR | TA | TA | TA | AR | AR |
| 1974 | TA | TA | GE | GE | CA | LE | LE | VI | LI | LI | SC | SA |
| 1975 | SA | CP | AQ | PI | PI | AR | TA | GE | GE | GE | CA | GE |

| | | |
|---|---|---|
| AR—Aries | LE—Leo | SA—Sagittarius |
| TA—Taurus | VI—Virgo | CP—Capricorn |
| GE—Gemini | LI—Libra | AQ—Aquarius |
| CA—Cancer | SC—Scorpio | PI—Pisces |

# 7

## Movers and Shakers:
## The Other Planets in Your Life

What astrology refers to as the "planets" are really moving bodies in the sky, which have been found to parallel certain types of events in our lives.

In forecasting, an astrologer will pay careful attention to how the planets relate to each other. For example, if two planets are in the same sign or opposite each other, they are going to have a definite impact on events in our individual lives and happenings in the world at large. We'll feel the positive force of those planets working together—or the tension and stress of them pulling in discordant directions.

One of the most curious phenomena in astrology is when the planets appear to move backward in the sky. This is known as a planet's *retrograde* motion. Actually, the planet is proceeding on its normal course, but, relative to our vantage point on the orbiting earth, which is circulating at a different speed, it looks to us like the planet has reversed direction (we simply have swung 'round the other side of the circle). But the apparent backward motion does affect us by stalling matters that the planet influences. During retrograde, it's time to reflect and review those matters and wait to proceed full speed ahead until we swing around in our orbit so that our movements are once again synchronized with those of that planet. Since all planets move at different speeds around the sun (except the moon, which is earth's satellite), they are all subject to periods of retrograde motion. The effects of a planet's retrograde period seem only natural when we consider that after every period of action, there should be a time to stop and reflect on what has been accomplished.

## The Personal Planets

The planets we have covered so far reveal the most about you. The sun is your basic personality. It dominates your horoscope; it is the basic color that touches and tinges everything else. The moon reveals your feelings, your cycle of emotional ups and downs. Venus tells how you react, and respond, and Mars shows your active aggressive nature. These are the most personal planets, the ones that really matter in your relationship with other people.

Just as each of the "personal" planets have distinct characteristics and roles to play, there are six more planets which astrologers consider. Some can be seen easily with the naked eye—others are dim mysterious bodies that reveal themselves only to the most powerful telescopes. These cold, distant planets take a long time to circle the sun. Pluto, the most remote, takes 248 years.

## Your Planetary Ruler

Each sun sign has a particular affinity for a special planet, which is called its "planetary ruler." In most cases, this identification of a planet with a sign evolved gradually over the centuries as the astrologers noted that the characteristics of a certain sign seemed to correspond with those of a planet.

Fiery, headstrong Aries is ruled by the active and aggressive planet Mars.

Sensual Taurus is ruled by beauty-loving Venus.

Verbal Gemini by Mercury, planet of communications.

Moody Cancer by the changeable Moon.

Regal Leo by the powerful Sun.

Critical analytical Virgo, also by Mercury.

Libra by the idealistic mental side of Venus.

Secretive, intense Scorpio by mysterious Pluto (also by forceful Mars).

Free-wheeling Sagittarius by fun-loving benevolent Jupiter.

Workaholic Capricorn by disciplined Saturn.

Unconventional Aquarius by brilliant unpredictible Uranus.

Creative, romantic Pisces by dreamy Neptune (also by generous Jupiter).

## Mercury . . . Your Planet of Communications

Mercury, the fastest moving planet and the one closest to the sun, whizzes through the zodiac in 88 days. It is so close to the sun that it never travels more than two zodiac signs away. This means you'll never find Mercury in a sign opposite your sun sign, working at cross-purposes.

This little planet, slightly larger than our moon, has always been identified with communications. It was once thought to bring messages from the powerful sun down to earth—sort of a secretary/ assistant to the sun. (And when something adversely affects Mercury, the whole office collapses!)

That's what happens to you when something affects your Mercury. Try as you might, you can't get things done. You miss your meeting, you get tied up in traffic, the plane is delayed, the computer breaks down. Or nobody really understands what you say or write. Messages get confused and misinterpreted.

What makes Mercury turn peevish? Usually it's a retrograde motion, which happens about three times a year. During those times, it's best to double-check everything (but sometimes even that won't help!). Go back over things, don't commit yourself to anything. Contracts signed under a Mercury retrograde are sure to be delayed.

Mercury will usually go retrograde in an element. (fire, earth, air, or water signs). This year the element is water, which means that three times this year, you'll have some snafus in your emotional communications which are water signs' territory. Be careful about declarations of undying love—you may regret them or change your mind when Mercury goes direct. Needless to say, the water signs (Cancer, Scorpio, and Pisces) will be especially vulnerable. These are the periods to watch in 1987 when Mercury goes retrograde:

February 18 to March 13 (retrograde in Pisces)
June 21 to July 7 (retrograde in Cancer)
October 16 to November 5 (retrograde in Scorpio)

Mercury rules the astrological signs of Virgo and Gemini, both signs who love to communicate, though in different ways. Gemini reflects the social aspects of Mercury, the wonderful way with words, the gift of gab, and the love of gossip. Virgo is the critical side of Mercury that loves to analyze, correct, and teach others.

Where Mercury appears in your horoscope determines how you communicate with others. If it is in the same sign as your sun, it will back up your sun sign's mental qualities. If it is in a different sign, it will reflect that other sign's qualities in your style of thinking, writing, and communicating. A Scorpio with Mercury in Scorpio might have a shrewd, stinging, penetrating style; however, if Mercury was in Libra, the Scorpio would reflect Libra's social grace, charm, and diplomacy.

**Jupiter . . . Luck and Expansion . . . Go for It!**
This enormous planet, 355 times larger than earth, is basically a huge ball of gaseous matter. It's jolly and jovial, sometimes not quite substantial, but it has always been associated with luck and happy

times, higher learning, lofty spiritual goals, a generous desire to improve the lot of your fellow man. Jupiter is the "good guy" of the zodiac, the hail-fellow-well-met, the one who gives you a loan or a raise.

Jupiter rules the sign of Sagittarius and is responsible for that sign's great sense of humor and love of fun and games. It is also responsible for Sag's lofty ideals and goals (which may also become as vaporous as the gassy consistency of the planet when it is time for them to materialize).

Under a good influence of Jupiter, it is time to expand. You'll expand your influence, your business, your mind, your waistline (!). When Jupiter enters your sun sign about every twelve years, it's time to cash in. This is when you get recognition, raises, attention. Good things come your way.

In 1987, Jupiter will be in Pisces during January and February and enter Aries on March 3.

**Saturn . . . Testing Time . . . Pull in Your Horns!**
Some would argue that astrologers are unfair to Saturn. Why should this huge (95 times as large as earth) spectacularly beautiful planet with its fascinating rings and moons be associated with such gloomy forecasts? Why isn't it the planet of love and beauty instead of Venus? Like Jupiter, this planet is easily observed with the naked eye, and since ancient times its movements have coincided with troubles and restrictions. But perhaps it is all in how you look at this planet. Saturn is a learning experience that makes you emerge from your testing time much the wiser.

A Saturn aspect makes you pull in your horns, stop, and think. It brings up questions of responsibility, duty, getting down to business, paying the bills. This stern taskmaster makes us deal with all those things that inevitably crop up that we love to postpone. We look forward to Saturn like an IRS investigation. But he's not such a bad guy. When Saturn tests us, he makes us examine our lives and appreciate things of value we may have taken for granted. If you have overextended yourself in any way, Saturn makes you face up and grow up. If your ambitions are making you lose sight of reality, Saturn brings things into focus.

The Saturn transits to watch are when Saturn is in your sun sign, when it is "squaring" your sun, and when it returns to its original place in your horoscope. The latter transit, called a "Saturn return" is most important because it usually signals a time of changes. Saturn orbits the sun every 29 years, so your first Saturn return comes at age 29, when many of us decide to settle down and finally face adult responsibilities. Under their first Saturn return, people change their attitudes about life— the playboy gets married, the vagabond settles down, the job-hopper focuses on a career, the career girl has a child. People get themselves together.

The second Saturn return at about age 58 usually marks the closing of the serious responsibilities of life, the relieving of the testing of Saturn. Hopefully, by this time you have learned the lessons of discipline, duty, and self-control that Saturn has taught you over the past 29 years.

In 1987 Saturn will spend the year in Sagittarius. So if Saturn was in Sagittarius at the time you were born or if your sun sign is Sagittarius, Gemini, Pisces, or Virgo, you will be feeling the "testing time" of Saturn.

## The Outer Planets—Uranus, Neptune, and Pluto

Far out in the solar system, these planets circle the sun slowly, spending a much longer time in each sign. Uranus spends about seven years in a sign, Neptune about 14 and Pluto can linger from 12 to 31 years in one sign. Therefore, the influence of these planets in a sign can color the personality and attitudes of the whole decade or generation born at the time. These planets are the planets of the "big picture," which have sweeping social, cultural, and spiritual influences.

Throughout your lifetime, as these planets move in their orbits, each will bring particular changes as it hits each sensitive spot in your horoscope. These transits are few and far between, but their effects are far-reaching. Here's what you can expect.

### Uranus . . . When Lightening Strikes!

Uranus is the planet that shakes you up with sudden and unexpected changes. It is connected with rebellion, uniqueness, and individuality—also, electronics, rock music, teengers, and the sign of Aquarius. A uranus transit begins the surprises that make life interesting.

You who are strongly influenced by Uranus are a little (or a lot) eccentric. You march to your own drummer and don't mind if some might find your life-style a bit shocking. Uranus challenges everyone to experiment, to risk, to leap forward, to make our own rules. During a Uranus transit, you'll get shaken up in some way, jolted out of a rut. You'll be extremely intuitive and, if you are willing to open your mind, to bend, and to try new things, you will find this one of the most exciting times of your life. You can expect the unexpected. But, if you persist in clinging to outmoded ideas or a rigid life-style, better fasten your seatbelt!

In 1987, Uranus continues its transit of Sagittarius, where it has been since 1981 and will remain until 1988. Obviously it affects Sagittarians most strongly. It will also shake up those signs in the square or opposition aspect: Pisces, Virgo, and Gemini. Your best strategy is to open your mind, experiment, and go where this erratic, never-dull planet leads you.

### Neptune . . . Your Dreams and Illusions

Neptune is about dreams, glamour, theater, illusions. It's no wonder that it rules films, perfumes, cosmetics—whatever fuels our fantasies. It also rules scheming, con games, and all manner of escapism, drugs, alcohol. Neptune is the planet of fantasies which can result in either self-deception or the most wonderful creativity.

It is also the planet of self-delusions. It is where you fool yourself, where you wear rose-colored glasses. In your chart it shows what makes you "high." It shows where you are idealistic, what *beyond* yourself interests you. Those with Neptune heavily aspected often have to choose between the devil and the deep blue sea and are often lured away from their goals by daydreams, fantasies, and visions of tropical islands.

Under a Neptune transit, you can become impractical, supersensitive, psychic, inspired, or self-destructive. It is a time when you are vulnerable and very easily deceived, but it can also be a time of great creativity, transformation, and spiritual growth.

Dreamy Neptune is currently in the stern sign of Capricorn and will remain there until 1998! This epoch will see a new fantasy oddly revolving around the very realistic Capricorn concerns: work, goals, success, tradition, and authority. Those born under Capricorn and signs at angles to Neptune will be Cancer; Aries and Libra will be feeling these Neptune vibrations strongly.

## Pluto . . . the Willpower Planet

Pluto represents the potential for death and rebirth, the energy that transforms you for better or for worse. This is the planet of inner housecleaning, it destroys in order to rebuild on a new foundation. A slow transit of Pluto over your sun or a key planet in your horoscope is sure to bring far-reaching and important changes in your life and your outlook. And after this cleansing, you emerge much clearer and more powerful, having thrown out the deadwood and perhaps made a complete change of direction.

In your birth horoscope, the sign and house of

your Pluto tells in which area of life you will strive against all odds, where you have willpower, where you will go to extremes.

This year, Pluto is continuing its long transit of Scorpio. Since it is the ruler of this sign, its infuence will be powerfully felt, effecting changes in medicine, science, police work, sexual mores and attitudes, and the military. Scorpios born from October 31 to November 4 will get the full impact. Taureans born April 28 to May 2 and Aquarians born January 28 to February 1 will also be feeling Pluto's power this year.

# 8

## Tapping the Planetary Power of Scorpio

Astrology is like a cosmic card game where every sign is dealt a special hand with powers that sum up the sign's essential character and can be played for better or for worse. Each sign gets an *element* and a *quality* (which we discussed in general in Chapter 1), a *position in the zodiac*, a special *planetary ruler*, and a *symbol* which reveals its deepest meaning. Let's learn how to play the Scorpio cards to make this a winning year for you.

### The Power of Your Element—Water

Scorpio's element is water, still waters that run deep. Yours is the sign that goes far beneath the surface of life. And since water symbolizes the emotions, you feel more deeply than others, and being hurt can be devastating. You care intensely about everything you do, which also makes you very vulnerable; everything sinks in, nothing rolls off your back. In your activities, you are meant to probe, to investigate, to penetrate the depths of emotions. You have the gift of insight for ferreting out secrets, for understanding unconscious motivations. But you very rarely show your own feelings, choosing to keep them safe beneath the surface, hidden in a cloak of mystery. Your challenge is to find a way to express the feeling, caring side of yourself in a constructive way,

## The Power of Your Quality—Fixed

The fixed quality of Scorpio gives you great determination and willpower. You go to extremes and often feel compelled to plumb the depths, to give all or nothing. But you know your own mind, and no one controls your opinions. You have great concentration and will see any situation through to the end, once you are committed. The fixed quality also makes you possessive and jealous, slow to change even when a new outlook will do you the most good. Your stubbornness can be your undoing, for you will not rest until the situation is resolved to your advantage, taking revenge when necessary. Your challenge is to learn when to persevere and when to bend or let go. Scorpios often self-destruct rather than feel that they have "lost" or been forced to give up control.

## The Power of Your Planetary Ruler—Pluto

Your planetary ruler is Pluto, the darkest, most mysterious planet of all. Discovered only in 1930 because of its strong gravitational pull on the orbit of Uranus, this tiny dense planet has come to represent power. And this is a major concern of those born under Scorpio. A Scorpio will know who's holding the reins—and how they got there. Like Pluto, Scorpios have strong personal magnetism that you often use to pull people in your chosen direction. It's Pluto's challenge to use your natural magnetism for the greater good, rather than for your own purposes. This darkest, most remote planet is named after the lord of the underworld, ruler of secret regions. It follows that Scorpio is the most secretive sign and finds it difficult to reveal its true feelings (you might lose control) and to trust anyone else. This distrust is often conveyed to others, who have an uneasy feeling about you. If you can show your sincere dedication and loyalty (you are the "rock of Gibraltar" and come through like a champion in times of crisis), you'll do much to improve your personal relationship.

## Your Position in the Zodiac—Eighth

The eighth position in the zodiac is concerned with death and regeneration; therefore, Scorpio is often compared to the phoenix who rises from the ashes. Nothing defeats you permanently. You have remarkable recuperative powers and can turn your life around after a serious setback. You also have the ability to transform others, to inspire them to change their lives for better or for worse. Like the late fall season, Scorpio tears down to prepare for rebuilding anew. In its most positive sense it is the necessary cleansing force that routes out problems, conquers disease, or probes the psyche. Negatively it can epitomize the misuse of power to destroy and control. The gifts of Scorpio are potent—it is your challenge to use them wisely.

## The Meaning of Your Symbol—Scorpion or Eagle

Your sign has two symbols: the scorpion, a poisonous insect that is capable of stinging itself to death, and the eagle, a noble bird that flies higher than any other. Scorpios have the ability to use their strong character to attain the heights or the depths of human experience. The shorthand symbol, or glyph, is a curving "M" shape which ends in a barbed arrow. The arrow is often taken for a phallic symbol. However, the sex experience for Scorpio is regenerative and revitalizing, not casual or promiscuous. You Scorpios are rarely casual about anything, especially sex. The glyph is more symbolic of Scorpio's use or misuse of power, and the barbed tail indicates either a destructive sting, or an arrow pointing to the eagle in the sky.

# 9

## The Scorpio Woman ...
## Man ... Child ... Spouse

### The Scorpio Woman

#### A Study in Contrasts

The Scorpio woman usually has two temperatures, icy cool and red hot. The cool Scorpio—Linda Evans and Grace Kelly are prime examples— smoulders far beneath the surface. To the public, she is a model of control and calm, deliberate action. The hot Scorpio—Katharine Hepburn and Vivien Leigh—is intense and demanding; she's got a strong personality that magnetizes everyone. She too is in control, but in an entirely different, very obvious way. Both types have in common, great self-discipline and dedication to everything they do. They are "all or nothing" types who often have a problem delegating authority and learning moderation.

Yet on the positive side, all this drive and need for control comes from the fact that the Scorpio woman cares deeply about everything she does—and everyone she chooses to involve herself with (and they will be few). It is important for her to turn her energies outward, to find fulfilling interests and a career, or she becomes the emotional "strangler"—too focused on too little.

## In Childhood

This is the quiet, self-contained child who rarely lets you know what she is thinking. But even so, you can sense that she knows exactly what she wants and how to get it. She's quick to spot others' weaknesses, and may use them to her advantage. She needs a great deal of love and affection and can be the most loyal and supportive of friends once they have earned her trust. Contact with boys is invigorating to her. She can be a great tomboy—the pal that hangs around with her brother's friends—and may choose some very masculine hobbies. But it is the power of the opposite sex that really intrigues her, and this is her way of getting some for herself. She may also become sexually precocious, intrigued with these powerful feelings. But even though she might be experimental, she'll keep under emotional control. Few Scorpios allow a male to take over.

## Growing Up

The Scorpio woman often finds the kind of warmth and affection she craves difficult to find. Superficial relationships rarely appeal to her. So she sometimes will substitute thrills and danger. Or she'll sublimate her needs by getting totally involved in a sport, a job, or studies. Her dedication to whatever she pursues soon earns her praise and attention—a far more certain source than fickle human relationships. One of her challenges is to learn to communicate her emotional needs to others. Either her cool or her self-sufficient facade, designed to hide her real, vulnerable feelings, is often too successful for her own good, and she deprives herself of real closeness to others.

## In Marriage

In the best marriage, the Scorpio finally finds someone to whom she can reveal her vulnerable feelings. Here she finds the closeness and approval she needs, and she rewards her husband with loyalty, devotion, competence, and intense sexuality. She's the organized superwife who can tackle many roles—career, wife, and mother—and make them all work. She does demand equal loyalty from her husband. Infidelity brings out her worst, retaliative characteristics. An overly domineering man is also a bad choice. Power struggles within the marriage deflect her naturally supportive caring tendencies. Scorpio is a sign that often will stick in an impossible situation rather than leave and admit defeat. She must learn when to cut her losses, for she has more resources than most to make a new start.

## As a Mother

This is a mother who either makes her children feel loved intensely or instills in them a guilt trip. She cares passionately about everything they do but often tries to program her children to do what she thinks is best for them. She may run into trouble if she has fire or air sign children who have their own ideas about what to do with their lives. In spite of her best-laid plans, the offspring will do their own thing. When a Scorpio's child goes out of control, she suffers great pangs of guilt. She needs to allow her children to find their own way, or they will spend much of their young lives reacting to her, rather than acting on their own.

## The Scorpio Man

### Lover of Power

The Scorpio man has a reputation of being the sexiest man in the zodiac. Not necessarily true. This man, though he is fascinated by sex, is interested because it is a powerful energizing force—and it is the power, not the passion that intrigues him. Scorpio is more about control. This is a man who never reveals his true motives. Something is always withheld, even when he seems most reckless, most abandoned.

The true Scorpio is a man who lives by self-control. Inside, he may be turbulent, but even the explosions you see are carefully calculated. For Scorpio, sexual activity is only the first layer of the onion. The real, vulnerable part of him is looking for a protective love, one who is so bound to him he need never fear rejection.

Scorpio is one of the most possessive signs of

the zodiac. These natives like to own what they own, with no questions, no doubts. Yet, paradoxically, they are always fascinated by the challenge, the hard-to-get. Like the Aries man, the Scorpio often finds himself in a double bind: The woman he can get and be sure of, is not enough of a challenge. And the unpredictable woman who fascinates him could possibly reject him. Until he learns to open up to someone to communicate as an equal, he's bound to play endless power games.

## In Childhood

Scorpio will withdraw into his own world rather than march to another's tune. Intensely curious, he has a scientific mind that will look to solve mysteries and find hidden meanings. He is strongly emotional and needs to find creative outlets rather than bottle himself up. This can be a very solitary secretive child, who must learn to open up, trust others, and risk hurt to grow. Little Scorpio also may demand privacy. He needs his own space where he feels safe from the prying of others. He must be encouraged to risk going out in the world, to try new things and risk rejection. A secure, demonstrative family can be of immeasureable help here.

## Growing Up

Scorpio discipline makes this young man excel at anything he does. He's not a "quick study," but he is more determined and thorough than anyone. He can be so focused on his goals that he ignores the human side of any situation. This is the consummate manipulator and user, who only sees others as a means to his end. He is unconcerned about others' opinion of him, especially if this might interfere with attaining his goals. Or it's the compassionate one who is determined to save the world, absolutely committed to a spiritual calling.

In personal relationships, Scorpio can use his unusual intuition and perception of others' weaknesses to control and dominate them. Or he can become focused on the object of his affection, fall truly and completely in love. He does, however, demand complete devotion from his beloved or forget it. He's the jealous type who will retaliate when challenged, with far more force than his lady ever imagined.

## In Marriage

Scorpio takes marriage as seriously as he does everything else. The right woman can give him great support and security, a nurturing haven, safe from the fear of rejection and of his own vulnerability. Hopefully, he will at last have the confidence to open up and share his deepest feelings. He is loyal to those few with whom he forms deep ties, despite continual temptations from the outside world. But this is a man who is constantly threatened, can be super-possessive and suspicious of a wife who insists on maintaining strong interests outside the home. She will need to make extra efforts to reassure him. When happily mated, however, the Scorpio will remain a devoted and passionate mate well into later years.

## As a Father

The Scorpio father can be a strict disciplinarian. He has strong opinions and may be overly stern with his children "for their own good." He's definitely the boss in the family, and even though he'll be anxious for them to be strong and independent, the lines of authority will be clearly drawn. His children won't get away with much. In their growing-up years, the children may be thankful for his firm guidance. But as they grow older, they often rebel or become "helpless" as they are intimidated by his power. The secret again, as in so many areas of Scorpio's life, is to learn to open up and reveal his human, caring, loving side—to give his children the solid self-esteem they need to grow strong and independent.

# 10

## Scorpio: Sign of Success

Did you ever wonder about the "Midas touch"? Why do some people seem to attract riches, fame, and success, while others seem to stay at the bottom of the heap, even though they work just as hard, may have just as much education and talent. Part of this "luck" surely has to do with being in the right place at the right time, but another part has to do with using the talents that come naturally where they will do the most good. If you find yourself continually frustrated in your career and money matters, perhaps the problem lies in your choice of work. Remember, success is not just material wealth and status, it is being happy and fulfilled in the kind of work you are doing.

There is no real "money" sign of the zodiac; there are millionaires born under every sign. But if we trace the so-called luck of many successful people, we can see that many have capitalized on the inner resources their sign has available. Your sign will find some kinds of work more congenial than others, or you may work best in a certain environment. For instance, a sociable Gemini might enjoy the bustle of a busy, noisy office, while a solitary Scorpio might prefer to work alone.

Some signs seem to work well independently; others prefer the structure of an organization. There are certain fields, too, that are more congenial to some signs than to others. There is an investment style that works well for you. For instance, a Taurus will want financial gains that are slow and steady and build permanent security, while a Sagittarian will get in and out fast, go for the short-term gain.

Here's a profile of Scorpio in the financial marketplace. Your best strategy is to understand your sign's strengths and weaknesses, look for a congenial field, and, if necessary, find a partner who has the strengths you lack: a supersalesman Leo to sell Cancer's inventive new product; a Capricorn to organize a Pisces. Remember, the stars are not the limit—it's how you use them that counts!

## Scorpio's Business Style

### How and Where Scorpio Works Best

Scorpio is a sign that puts itself on the line, to win or to lose. Yet, you'll minimize your risk by thoroughly researching all the angles. You have the guts to try almost anything, providing it gives you a sense of power and control if you win. You are a sign that goes to extremes: Intense and magnetic, you give all or nothing. This may make life a bit trying on a day-to-day basis. You need to learn moderation, establish priorities, and delegate responsibilities. You have great discipline and capacity for work, you don't stop till the job is done. Yet, on the negative side, you may take your task too seriously, work too intensely, and be too demanding of others. You need a job atmosphere that gives you the promise of control, of running your own show, and that offers a challenge to your penetrating mind.

## Scorpio's Best Careers

Find a job that takes advantage of your probing, investigative nature. You see through to the core of a problem, which makes you a natural psychoanalyst, detective, research scientist, strategist, or tax investigator. In fact, any job that requires problem-solving is a natural for you. Your attraction for situations involving discipline, power, and control could draw you into police work, martial arts, the military. Or your need to be on the edge of life or death could make you a super obstetrician, surgeon, funeral director, or emergency room attendant. Creatively you set the lasting classic styles as many top fashion designers and models can demonstrate. And your sensual magnetism radiates from the theater or TV screen.

## Scorpio as Boss

A Scorpio boss usually makes his or her position clear by being in total control of every situation. You draw definite lines over which your underlings dare not step. Yet you care deeply about every project; you'll tackle every problem, endure the most difficult office politics to accomplish your goals. Your problem is that your underlings may not approach each task with the same fervor that you do. Clearly stated goals can help remedy the situation. Another problem is your great reserve: Others sense you're holding back and may not trust you completely. Your calm mask of poise and control may actually backfire. Learn to share yourself with others, open up more, and turn your gaze outward. You'll find others will let down their guard too; you'll get even more accomplished.

## Scorpio as Employee

You're the cool, calm, and collected eye of the storm, the one who can be counted on to hang in there under the toughest pressure. It's as if you were born to be on the firing line, and you were! You almost thrive under extreme circumstances, life-or-death situations. It's important to find a job that has this challenge, this slight element of danger, and the potential to gain power and control. You want to be the one the organization depends on. You usually study the dynamics of each situation intently, learn who wields the power, and what your chances are to get a piece of the action. And you're not above doing a bit of manipulation to get where you want. You're dead serious about your goals. Loosen up a bit! By rationing your powerful drive, you'll get to your destination even faster!

# 11

## Making the Most of Your Scorpio Love Nature

### Is There a Right Sign for You?

Finding Mr. or Ms. Right is one of the main reasons people turn to astrology. We are fascinated by how accurate an astrologer's appraisal of our own wants and needs can be. And if you hope to attract a special person, it can be valuable to know that there are certain qualities you can expect from him or her and others you should not expect. You'll be pleasantly surprised if these qualities occur anyway, but you won't be disappointed if they don't.

On the other hand, some of you might be in a relationship which started out blissfully, then took a turn for the worse. Astrology can warn you when compatible signs might turn sour and give you the secret why odd couples work beautifully. Again, much depends on your expectations. If you are expecting a Sagittarius to be a happy homebody, or a Leo to be thrifty, you may be undermining the relationship. Astrology can help you accentuate the positive factors of each sign instead, to enjoy the Sagittarian's wonderful sense of humor and sociability and to revel in the star quality of the Leo.

Under the chapters dealing with the moon, Mars, and Venus, it was emphasized that astrology considers many factors other than sun signs to determine the compatibility of two people. Though the sun is the center around which all of our activity revolves, the moon (our emotional nature), Mars (our active sexuality), and Venus (our re-active side: what turns us on) are also very important. So are the influences on the seventh house, that part of each horoscope that rules marriage and partnership. Supposedly incompatible sun signs can work out beautifully together if other aspects are in tune.

Your sun may be the only planet in its sign, or it may be accompanied by other planets, which will make the influence of that sign on your personality even stronger. A sun and Venus in the sign of Capricorn will make that person a much more obvious Capricorn than if the sun were alone.

When you share the same sun sign with someone, you should feel very comfortable with them, at first. You should agree on many things, because you have much in common. You'll understand and be sympathetic with this person's qualities, you feel like soul mates. After a while, however, you may get a bit bored, unless there are other aspects in your horoscopes to provide a challenge and expand your horizons.

With a sign in the "square" or opposition aspect (three or six signs away) you might feel a bit antagonistic initially, then a sexy chemistry will happen and sparks will fly! Later on, you may find that your differences continue to fascinate each other: You're never bored!

Here are the pros and cons of each sun sign as it relates to yours. But bear in mind that harmony and stimulation are balanced in most successful and long-lasting relationships. Too smooth a relationship can result in boredom, too much excitement and stimulation in exhaustion and burnout. Everyone must recognize his or her need for balance and also for the constructive challenges that make us grow. The pros, areas of interest and harmony, are contrasted with the cons where you will challenge and teach each other.

### Scorpio–Aries

PROS: You are both ruled by Mars and therefore can generate great power together. You both admire each other's stamina, bravery, and courage in the face of great odds. You challenge and stimulate each other—both of you love a dare, and you may just try this one on for size!

CONS: Open Aries never quite understands what secretive Scorpio is really up to. You are both overly jealous and like to control; Aries pushes to get his or her way while Scorpio plots, schemes, and stings. A power struggle between you two can be a real tug of war, with Aries launching a frontal attack, while Scorpio counters with guerrilla tactics and sabotage. Later, Scorpio will hold a grudge and seek revenge, while Aries tends to hit and run.

### Scorpio–Taurus
PROS: A great love match where Scorpio intensity blends with Taurean sensuality. Both of you are committed types who never stray unless truly miserable. Taurus admires Scorpio's thoroughness and insight, while their steady calm emotional nature soothes Scorpio's inner turbulence.

CONS: Scorpios can be devious and secretive, which Taurus mistrusts. Both of you can be manipulative and stubborn. It's better to deal with questions of power, territory, and control as soon as possible in the relationship. And accept the fact that you won't really control each other.

### Scorpio–Gemini
PROS: Gemini's many phases and faces fascinate Scorpio. Gemini's lighthearted wit and charm lifts them out of their darker moods, yet, tantalizingly to Scorpio, Gemini can never be possessed. Gemini's versatility and Scorpio's powerful intensity is stimulating and creative. Scorpio can make those Gemini ideas happen!

CONS: Scorpio likes to have everything under control, which sounds like prison to Gemini. And, to make this relationship work, Gemini must stay true blue or risk a jealous Scorpio sting. This may cramp Gemini's gadabout life-style. When Scorpio gets "heavy" emotionally, Gemini usually takes flight.

## Scorpio–Cancer

PROS: A great match (à la Prince Charles and Princess Di). Cancer's caring instincts make intense, passionate Scorpios feel secure. They are both extremely possessive. Scorpio's need to control and self-discipline finds a good mate in the shrewd, self-protective Cancer. This works equally well in business and romance.

CONS: Clinging Cancers can cause a Scorpio to want to break loose. And Scorpio's black moods can coincide with the darker side of Cancer. In which case, no one comes to the rescue. Both want everything from their lover, but always hold a bit of themselves in reserve.

## Scorpio–Leo

PROS: The chemistry is powerful between the regal warmhearted Leo and the magnetic intense Scorpio. You approach each other with mutual respect. The possessive Scorpio gives Leo the attention this sign needs, while Leo brings the secretive Scorpion out into the sunshine. You are both achievers who can truly appreciate each other.

CONS: Careful with power struggles here! You are two dangerous adversaries who like to control his or her own territory and sometimes step over the boundaries. Leo is open and dramatic in articulating needs, but Scorpio rarely tells you the real story. Scorpio may also try to control the budget, which can turn the warmhearted spendthrift Leo ice cold.

## Scorpio–Virgo

PROS: Virgo can live out those secret fantasies

with a passionate Scorpio. Though both of you can appear rather cool on the surface, you know there are turbulent inner emotions. You both demand and deliver fidelity, unless there are serious problems to send you scurrying elsewhere. Scorpio can take control while Virgo handles the details. Both of you appreciate each other's discipline and dedication.

CONS: When Virgo nags, Scorpio stings. Scorpio sometimes plays emotional games which try Virgo's patience and upset their digestion. Scorpio's secretive nature irritates Virgo, who may feel there is something not quite trustworthy about the person.

### Scorpio–Libra

PROS: Scorpios provide the intensity and decisiveness that Libra lacks. And the Libran charm lightens Scorpio's dark moods. Scorpio may also be challenged by Libra's emotional coolness, especially if you play hard-to-get. Libra's taste and good looks are a social asset to Scorpio.

CONS: Scorpio's possessiveness and desire to control could set the Libran scales off balance. And if Libra starts to flirt, Scorpio may retaliate with a jealous sting. Scorpio's heavy-handedness may be a turn-off to refined, diplomatic Librans. Scorpio may also be disappointed to discover that Librans are rarely passionately committed to anyone.

### Scorpio–Scorpio

PROS: Here is a couple that can stick together through thick and thin. It's a sizzling combination where each understands the other's intense needs yet has no fear of them. You are both secretive types who love a good mystery and will find it in each other.

CONS: Everything augurs well, as long as you avoid a power struggle. Scorpios love to control, but never to be controlled. Neither of you ever gives in, so battles can rage on indefinitely, with neither able to forgive, forget, and start over. You also have to be careful not to be too wound up in each other. Let the rest of the world in from time to time to give you fresh air and inspiration.

### Scorpio–Sagittarius
PROS: Jovial Sagittarius are perfect for brightening up Scorpios' lives. They are the perennial optimists and their can-do attitude encourages Scorpios to soar like an eagle, and maybe make some high-flying Sagittarian ideas happen. You both love the great outdoors, competitive sports, and exotic, erotic adventures. Sag can teach Scorpio a more philosophical point of view—not to take life so seriously.

CONS: Scorpion intensity is no joke. Sag must learn that Scorpios are not to be trifled with. A hit-and-run romance could leave Sag with permanent injury. You will also have to learn not to arouse Scorpio's jealousy. In turn, Scorpio will have to come out of its shell, share some fun and games, and suffer in silence.

### Scorpio–Capricorn
PROS: you are both hard-working and ambitious,

with your sights set on high goals and the discipline and practical know-how to get there. You feel very comfortable with each other and you manage to avoid power struggles. You are both loners who understand each other's need for private time.

CONS: Both of you have dark moods when you're best left alone. Hopefully, they won't coincide. There's also the possibility that you both may focus on work goals and have little time for each other. You need to deliberately make time together to find outlets that lift your spirits.

### Scorpio–Aquarius

PROS: The chemistry between you is electric. Aquarius' inventiveness and originality turn Scorpio on. Your scientific minds devise some fascinating experiments together. Scorpio helps Aquarius live your far-out fantasies. Both of you need your own space and respect each other's ideals and values.

CONS: Aquarius likes to be up front, Scorpio prefers behind the scenes. Aquarius demands unfettered freedom and needs an anchor, not a noose. Aquarian's impersonal "friend of the world" attitude may seem superficial to Scorpios who look for emotional depth. You may need security just when Aquarius needs space.

### Scorpio–Pisces

PROS: This can be a long-running romance. Scorpio and Pisces live in emotional water and can plumb the depths together. Piscean creativity flourishes under Scorpio's organizational power, while the Scorpion intensity gives Pisces the security and ballast this sensitive sign needs. Pisces instinctively knows how to lift Scorpio's darker moods and the lovemaking is star quality.

CONS: Pisceans can seem gentle and malleable, but this independent sign resents rules and orders. If Scorpio decides to exercise too much control, Pisces slips away. Both are prone to negative moods and understand how to manipulate each other to get their way.

# 12

## The Impression You Make:
## Your Rising Sign

Can people guess your sun sign soon after meeting you? Or do they say: "You seem so sociable for a Scorpio," or "You look more like a Leo," or "You're so conservative; I thought Scorpios were supposed to look sexy." Though your sun sign characteristics sooner or later shine through, the first impression you make may be quite the contrary. This is because your rising sign (or ascendant) is temporarily taking over.

Your rising sign or ascendant is the sign on the eastern horizon at the exact moment of birth. Because this is the moment that begins your independent life, when you first assert yourself, it follows that your rising sign is a major influence on how you first appear to others. It determines your outward personality, your style, the way you express yourself naturally. It can even influence your physical appearance: the color of your hair, the way you walk, your bone structure.

In order to find the exact degree of your rising sign, you must know your exact time of birth since the degree of a rising sign changes every four minutes. However, if you know, within two hours, your time of birth, you can make a very good guess at your rising sign with the help of the chart in Chapter 13. If your appearance and mannerisms do not tally up with the description of your ascendant in this chapter, look at the description of the signs immediately preceding and following. Chances are, your timing may be an hour or so off, and one of these other rising signs will be more like your image.

Many people were born early in the morning, when the sun was rising. This means your rising sign is the same as your sun sign. It will reinforce the outward qualities of your sun sign; you'll have double your sun's charisma. And chances are, other astrology-conscious people will be able to identify your sign right away.

An ascendant in a different sign will color your sun sign's characteristics with its special qualities. A shy Cancer with supersalesman Sagittarius rising will project jovial good humor; a Virgo with Scorpio rising will have Scorpio sex appeal coloring the prim Virgo manner.

Here's how the different rising signs color the basic Scorpio personality:

**Scorpio with Aries rising:**    There's nothing subtle about you. You come on strong, assertive, and aggressive—perhaps even belligerent. Learn to tone it down, or life will seem like a series of confrontations. You're the type who won't take no for an answer.

**Scorpio with Taurus rising:** You're almost too sweet and sexy for your own good. You project soft sensuality, but there's a core of discipline underneath. You're stubborn and slow to change your mind. You move slowly, have a beautiful voice, and may tend to overindulge in everything. Watch your weight.

**Scorpio with Gemini rising:** You're charming and talkative—but not about your real concerns. This superficial gift of gab conceals your deeply emotional nature. People are surprised at your intensity when they get to know you. Physically, you're slim and animated, with expressive hands.

**Scorpio with Cancer rising:** You appear to be shy and brooding and very secretive. You tend to throw a self-protective screen about you and rarely say directly what you want. You may have a very seductive curvacious body, which tends to be overweight.

**Scorpio with Leo rising:** You give the appearance of power personified. You seem to walk in and command attention. You have an open, positive, commanding manner with theatrical gestures. Beautiful hair and a cleft chin are other gifts of this rising sign.

**Scorpio with Virgo rising:**    You are a fault-finder *extraordinaire*. Nothing escapes your eagle eye. You seem to be intolerant of other's imperfections. Learn to temper your criticisms with diplomacy. Show you care.

**Scorpio with Libra rising:**    You're cool and charming, with a beautiful smile. You are probably very good looking and fascinating to the opposite sex. You pay great attention to dress and grooming and present an impression of calm and balance that belies your inner intensity.

**Scorpio with Scorpio rising:**    You double Scorpios play up your air of mystery. No one can guess what is really going on with you. Yet your intensity and magnetism fascinates others, expecially those of the opposite sex. You seem never to do anything halfway.

**Scorpio with Sagittarius rising:**    You're more bouncy and jovial than the typical Scorpio. You are probably very athletic and well coordinated. You tend to be very blunt, however. Temper your frankness with a sense of humor.

**Scorpio with Capricorn rising:**    You know how to look and act rich. You could easily come across as a snob. People tend to defer to you as if you were the boss. You have strong bone structure and a rather melancholy expression, with lovely, rather sad eyes.

**Scorpio with Aquarius rising:** You can seem very distant and cool, interested in life's more esoteric matters. You can be very psychic and mysterious; some of you seem quite far out. You prefer to deal with people in groups. It is difficult to feel close to you.

**Scorpio with Pisces rising:** You're a great actor that seems to change personalities at a moment's notice, never revealing your true self. This makes you seem a bit untrustworthy. But you have great sex appeal and beautiful eyes that win over many.

# 13

## Find Your Rising Sign

It is easier than many people think to find out your rising sign. One reason is that it is based on "universal" or "sidereal" time—the measure used in space travel. To ascertain your rising sign, look through the following chart and locate the birthdate nearest your birth date; look across and locate the time nearest your birth time. Remember that if daylight saving time was in effect at your birth, you must subtract one hour from the time stated on your birth certificate. In the section for your date and time, you will find an abbreviation for the sign that was rising when you were born. For instance, if your birthdate is June 12 at 9:30 a.m., your rising sign is Leo; if you were born on the same date at 9:30 p.m., your rising sign is Capricorn.

You will notice that the *year* you were born does not affect your rising sign. However, the geographical latitude does. These tables are calculated for the middle latitudes of the United States. If you were born far to the south, it is wise to look at the sign that *follows* your rising sign as well. If you were born far to the north, check out the *previous* sign.

# Rising Signs—A.M. Births

| | 1 AM | 2 AM | 3 AM | 4 AM | 5 AM | 6 AM | 7 AM | 8 AM | 9 AM | 10 AM | 11 AM | 12 NOON |
|---|---|---|---|---|---|---|---|---|---|---|---|---|
| Jan 1 | Lib | Sc | Sc | Sc | Sag | Sag | Cap | Cap | Aq | Aq | Pis | Ar |
| Jan 9 | Lib | Sc | Sc | Sag | Sag | Sag | Cap | Cap | Aq | Pis | Ar | Tau |
| Jan 17 | Sc | Sc | Sc | Sag | Sag | Cap | Cap | Aq | Aq | Pis | Ar | Tau |
| Jan 25 | Sc | Sc | Sag | Sag | Sag | Cap | Cap | Aq | Pis | Ar | Tau | Tau |
| Feb 2 | Sc | Sc | Sag | Sag | Cap | Cap | Aq | Pis | Pis | Ar | Tau | Gem |
| Feb 10 | Sc | Sag | Sag | Sag | Cap | Cap | Aq | Pis | Ar | Tau | Tau | Gem |
| Feb 18 | Sc | Sag | Sag | Cap | Cap | Aq | Pis | Pis | Ar | Tau | Gem | Gem |
| Feb 26 | Sag | Sag | Sag | Cap | Aq | Aq | Pis | Ar | Tau | Tau | Gem | Gem |
| Mar 6 | Sag | Sag | Cap | Cap | Aq | Pis | Pis | Ar | Tau | Gem | Gem | Cap |
| Mar 14 | Sag | Cap | Cap | Aq | Aq | Pis | Ar | Tau | Tau | Gem | Gem | Can |
| Mar 22 | Sag | Cap | Cap | Aq | Pis | Ar | Ar | Tau | Gem | Gem | Can | Can |
| Mar 30 | Cap | Cap | Aq | Pis | Pis | Ar | Tau | Tau | Gem | Can | Can | Can |
| Apr 7 | Cap | Cap | Aq | Pis | Ar | Ar | Tau | Gem | Gem | Can | Can | Leo |
| Apr 14 | Cap | Aq | Aq | Pis | Ar | Tau | Tau | Gem | Gem | Can | Can | Leo |
| Apr 22 | Cap | Aq | Pis | Ar | Ar | Tau | Gem | Gem | Gem | Can | Leo | Leo |
| Apr 30 | Aq | Aq | Pis | Ar | Tau | Tau | Gem | Can | Can | Can | Leo | Leo |
| May 8 | Aq | Pis | Ar | Ar | Tau | Gem | Gem | Can | Can | Leo | Leo | Leo |
| May 16 | Aq | Pis | Ar | Tau | Gem | Gem | Can | Can | Can | Leo | Leo | Vir |
| May 24 | Pis | Ar | Ar | Tau | Gem | Gem | Can | Can | Leo | Leo | Leo | Vir |
| June 1 | Ar | Ar | Tau | Gem | Gem | Can | Can | Can | Leo | Leo | Vir | Vir |
| June 9 | Ar | Ar | Tau | Gem | Gem | Can | Can | Leo | Leo | Leo | Vir | Vir |
| June 17 | Ar | Tau | Gem | Gem | Can | Can | Can | Leo | Leo | Vir | Vir | Vir |
| June 25 | Tau | Tau | Gem | Gem | Can | Can | Leo | Leo | Leo | Vir | Vir | Lib |
| July 3 | Tau | Gem | Gem | Can | Can | Can | Leo | Leo | Vir | Vir | Vir | Lib |
| July 11 | Tau | Gem | Gem | Can | Can | Leo | Leo | Leo | Vir | Vir | Lib | Lib |
| July 18 | Gem | Gem | Can | Can | Can | Leo | Leo | Vir | Vir | Vir | Lib | Lib |
| July 26 | Gem | Gem | Can | Can | Leo | Leo | Vir | Vir | Vir | Lib | Lib | Lib |
| Aug 3 | Gem | Can | Can | Can | Leo | Leo | Vir | Vir | Vir | Lib | Lib | Sc |
| Aug 11 | Gem | Can | Can | Leo | Leo | Leo | Vir | Vir | Lib | Lib | Lib | Sc |
| Aug 18 | Can | Can | Can | Leo | Leo | Vir | Vir | Vir | Lib | Lib | Sc | Sc |
| Aug 27 | Can | Can | Leo | Leo | Leo | Vir | Vir | Lib | Lib | Lib | Sc | Sc |
| Sept 4 | Can | Can | Leo | Leo | Leo | Vir | Vir | Vir | Lib | Lib | Sc | Sc |
| Sept 12 | Can | Leo | Leo | Leo | Vir | Vir | Lib | Lib | Lib | Sc | Sc | Sag |
| Sept 30 | Leo | Leo | Leo | Vir | Vir | Vir | Lib | Lib | Sc | Sc | Sc | Sag |
| Sept 28 | Leo | Leo | Leo | Vir | Vir | Lib | Lib | Lib | Sc | Sc | Sag | Sag |
| Oct 6 | Leo | Leo | Vir | Vir | Vir | Lib | Lib | Sc | Sc | Sc | Sag | Sag |
| Oct 14 | Leo | Vir | Vir | Vir | Lib | Lib | Lib | Sc | Sc | Sag | Sag | Cap |
| Oct 22 | Leo | Vir | Vir | Lib | Lib | Lib | Sc | Sc | Sc | Sag | Sag | Cap |
| Oct 30 | Vir | Vir | Vir | Lib | Lib | Sc | Sc | Sc | Sag | Sag | Cap | Cap |
| Nov 7 | Vir | Vir | Lib | Lib | Lib | Sc | Sc | Sc | Sag | Sag | Cap | Cap |
| Nov 15 | Vir | Vir | Lib | Lib | Sc | Sc | Sc | Sag | Sag | Cap | Cap | Aq |
| Nov 23 | Vir | Lib | Lib | Lib | Sc | Sc | Sag | Sag | Sag | Cap | Cap | Aq |
| Dec 1 | Vir | Lib | Lib | Sc | Sc | Sc | Sag | Sag | Cap | Cap | Aq | Aq |
| Dec 9 | Lib | Lib | Lib | Sc | Sc | Sag | Sag | Sag | Cap | Cap | Aq | Pis |
| Dec 18 | Lib | Lib | Sc | Sc | Sc | Sag | Sag | Cap | Cap | Aq | Aq | Pis |
| Dec 28 | Lib | Lib | Sc | Sc | Sag | Sag | Sag | Cap | Aq | Aq | Pis | Ar |

# Rising Signs—P.M. Births

| | 1 PM | 2 PM | 3 PM | 4 PM | 5 PM | 6 PM | 7 PM | 8 PM | 9 PM | 10 PM | 11 PM | 12 MIDNIGHT |
|---|---|---|---|---|---|---|---|---|---|---|---|---|
| Jan 1 | Tau | Gem | Gem | Can | Can | Can | Leo | Leo | Vir | Vir | Vir | Lib |
| Jan 9 | Tau | Gem | Gem | Can | Can | Leo | Leo | Leo | Vir | Vir | Vir | Lib |
| Jan 17 | Gem | Gem | Can | Can | Can | Leo | Leo | Vir | Vir | Vir | Lib | Lib |
| Jan 25 | Gem | Gem | Can | Can | Leo | Leo | Leo | Vir | Vir | Lib | Lib | Lib |
| Feb 2 | Gem | Can | Can | Can | Leo | Leo | Vir | Vir | Vir | Lib | Lib | Sc |
| Feb 10 | Gem | Can | Can | Can | Leo | Leo | Vir | Vir | Vir | Lib | Lib | Sc |
| Feb 18 | Can | Can | Can | Leo | Leo | Vir | Vir | Vir | Lib | Lib | Sc | Sc |
| Feb 26 | Can | Can | Leo | Leo | Leo | Vir | Vir | Lib | Lib | Lib | Sc | Sc |
| Mar 6 | Can | Leo | Leo | Leo | Vir | Vir | Vir | Lib | Lib | Sc | Sc | Sc |
| Mar 14 | Can | Leo | Leo | Vir | Vir | Vir | Lib | Lib | Lib | Sc | Sc | Sag |
| Mar 22 | Leo | Leo | Leo | Vir | Vir | Lib | Lib | Lib | Sc | Sc | Sc | Sag |
| Mar 30 | Leo | Leo | Vir | Vir | Vir | Lib | Lib | Sc | Sc | Sc | Sag | Sag |
| Apr 7 | Leo | Leo | Vir | Vir | Lib | Lib | Lib | Sc | Sc | Sc | Sag | Sag |
| Apr 14 | Leo | Vir | Vir | Vir | Lib | Lib | Sc | Sc | Sc | Sag | Sag | Cap |
| Apr 22 | Leo | Vir | Vir | Lib | Lib | Lib | Sc | Sc | Sc | Sag | Sag | Cap |
| Apr 30 | Vir | Vir | Vir | Lib | Lib | Sc | Sc | Sc | Sag | Sag | Cap | Cap |
| May 8 | Vir | Vir | Lib | Lib | Lib | Sc | Sc | Sag | Sag | Sag | Cap | Cap |
| May 16 | Vir | Vir | Lib | Lib | Sc | Sc | Sc | Sag | Sag | Cap | Cap | Aq |
| May 24 | Vir | Lib | Lib | Lib | Sc | Sc | Sag | Sag | Sag | Cap | Cap | Aq |
| June 1 | Vir | Lib | Lib | Sc | Sc | Sc | Sag | Sag | Cap | Cap | Aq | Aq |
| June 9 | Lib | Lib | Lib | Sc | Sc | Sag | Sag | Sag | Cap | Cap | Aq | Pis |
| June 17 | Lib | Lib | Sc | Sc | Sc | Sag | Sag | Cap | Cap | Aq | Aq | Pis |
| June 25 | Lib | Lib | Sc | Sc | Sag | Sag | Sag | Cap | Cap | Aq | Pis | Ar |
| July 3 | Lib | Sc | Sc | Sc | Sag | Sag | Cap | Cap | Aq | Aq | Pis | Ar |
| July 11 | Lib | Sc | Sc | Sag | Sag | Sag | Cap | Cap | Aq | Aq | Pis | Tau |
| July 18 | Sc | Sc | Sc | Sag | Sag | Cap | Cap | Aq | Aq | Pis | Ar | Tau |
| July 26 | Sc | Sc | Sag | Sag | Sag | Cap | Cap | Aq | Pis | Ar | Tau | Tau |
| Aug 3 | Sc | Sc | Sag | Sag | Cap | Cap | Aq | Aq | Pis | Ar | Tau | Gem |
| Aug 11 | Sc | Sag | Sag | Sag | Cap | Cap | Aq | Pis | Ar | Tau | Tau | Gem |
| Aug 18 | Sc | Sag | Sag | Cap | Cap | Aq | Pis | Pis | Ar | Tau | Gem | Gem |
| Aug 28 | Sag | Sag | Sag | Cap | Cap | Aq | Pis | Ar | Tau | Tau | Gem | Gem |
| Sept 4 | Sag | Sag | Cap | Cap | Aq | Pis | Pis | Ar | Tau | Gem | Gem | Can |
| Sept 12 | Sag | Sag | Cap | Aq | Aq | Pis | Ar | Tau | Tau | Gem | Gem | Can |
| Sept 20 | Sag | Cap | Cap | Aq | Pis | Pis | Ar | Tau | Gem | Gem | Can | Can |
| Sept 28 | Cap | Cap | Aq | Aq | Pis | Ar | Tau | Tau | Gem | Gem | Can | Can |
| Oct 6 | Cap | Cap | Aq | Pis | Ar | Ar | Tau | Gem | Gem | Can | Can | Leo |
| Oct 14 | Cap | Aq | Aq | Pis | Ar | Tau | Tau | Gem | Gem | Can | Can | Leo |
| Oct 22 | Cap | Aq | Pis | Ar | Ar | Tau | Gem | Gem | Can | Can | Leo | Leo |
| Oct 30 | Aq | Aq | Pis | Ar | Tau | Tau | Gem | Can | Can | Can | Leo | Leo |
| Nov 7 | Aq | Aq | Pis | Ar | Tau | Tau | Gem | Can | Can | Can | Leo | Leo |
| Nov 15 | Aq | Pis | Ar | Tau | Gem | Gem | Can | Can | Can | Leo | Leo | Vir |
| Nov 23 | Pis | Ar | Ar | Tau | Gem | Gem | Can | Can | Leo | Leo | Leo | Vir |
| Dec 1 | Pis | Ar | Tau | Gem | Gem | Can | Can | Can | Leo | Leo | Vir | Vir |
| Dec 9 | Ar | Tau | Tau | Gem | Gem | Can | Can | Leo | Leo | Leo | Vir | Vir |
| Dec 18 | Ar | Tau | Gem | Gem | Can | Can | Can | Leo | Leo | Vir | Vir | Vir |
| Dec 28 | Tau | Tau | Gem | Gem | Can | Can | Leo | Leo | Vir | Vir | Vir | Lib |

# 14

---

## Scorpio Astro-Outlook for 1987

Love and marriage could be on the agenda this year, Scorpio. Whatever you do, you'll search for greater harmony, balance, and beauty—either in existing relationships or in new, fulfilling romances. Before you settle down to a placid existence, however, you may be called upon to clear away deep resentments from the past. This is not always easy for you, Scorpio, but the rewards will make it all worthwhile.

You'll be sprucing up home and property— possibly preparing for a family reunion, anniversary, or wedding. If your present quarters are undesirable, you might seriously consider a change in residence, a renovation project, or a complete redecoration of your home, tossing away items that remind you of the past.

During the past few years, many of your ideas and formerly fixed opinions have been changing. This may be reflected in your surroundings, personality, physical appearance, or even marital status. Dreams and ideals color your thinking; your psychic perceptions deepen; you "go out on a limb" with friends and neighbors as you express interest in the spiritual and the occult.

You'll have mixed feelings about money and spending and could benefit from windfalls and original ideas, but will be willing to work hard, at the same time, to save and preserve for the future.

In March, Jupiter begins to favorably influence employment, health, dependents, pets, and service to others and will continue to do so for the remainder of the year. April, when new starts of all kinds are accented, you'll hear news about a job, promotion, or another lucky break to do with your work. But don't ignore the months of February and November for getting ahead in love, money, prestige, and gaining the rewards you've truly earned. June and August are especially good for travel, adventure, and increased communication with someone you love or admire.

As always, periods when the sun is in your own sign (October 23–November 21), in Pisces (February 20– March 20), or in Cancer (June 22–July 21) are especially fortunate. You'll also be at your seductive, charming best when Venus is in Scorpio this year (January 1–6 and October 11–November 3).

For greater details about the year ahead, please turn to your day-by-day forecasts in the following pages.

# 15

## Fifteen Months of Day-by-Day Predictions

### OCTOBER 1986

**Wednesday, October 1 (Moon in Virgo)**  Someone may try to rattle you today, and even try to make you "jump through hoops." Stand your ground and refuse to show that it gets to you; use that famous Scorpio reserve. Later on, you should find yourself in very good company having a very good time. Just don't go overboard with foreign or exotic food. Pamper your digestion.

**Thursday, October 2 (Moon Virgo to Libra 8:03 p.m.)**  Now your firm stance of the past few days pays off for you. Things are clicking right along, and your judgment is very keen. Someone may seek you out today and ask you to make an evaluation of a personal situation; be fair, but make it clear that you can't get involved. The lucky number is 8.

***Friday, October 3 (Moon in Libra)*** As the work week winds down, you may feel yourself in need of pampering. Do something for yourself—but include others too. Your sense of the beautiful will be very stimulated now, and you may find music particularly soothing. Don't allow yourself to feel "left out" if you aren't invited somewhere.

***Saturday, October 4 (Moon Libra to Scorpio 11:35 p.m.)*** You probably would be happiest if you didn't have to go anywhere today; your mood is more or less "I want to be alone." Use this quiet time to sort out some things—both mental and material. You could make more room for new "acquisitions." Try your luck with number 1.

***Sunday, October 5 (Moon in Scorpio)*** What a feeling! You should wake ready for anything—well, almost anything. Don't get too carried away with physical exercise, because you could drive yourself beyond your limit. Instead, use all that vigor to "score points" with someone around you who expresses a lot of interest. It could prove interesting.

***Monday, October 6 (Moon in Scorpio)*** Accept a last-minute invitation to an event you didn't expect to attend; don't let pride get in your way. Ride with the tide, and take the initiative today; you have every reason to be absolutely confident. The lucky number today could be 3.

***Tuesday, October 7 (Moon Scorpio to Sagittarius 1:48 a.m.)*** Your thoughts are very much on your financial situation today, and how to increase your income potential. By being cautiously speculative, you could strike on just the right things. Keep on forging ahead, because your cycle is quite high. Someone will give you a compliment that means more than money.

**Wednesday, October 8 (Moon in Sagittarius)** Something you thought was totally out of reach is now there for the taking. When you express your elation, don't let anyone throw a wet blanket over you. Keep your eyes on the stars, and keep negativity out of your scheme of things. Sometimes you lack the natural optimism of other people.

**Thursday, October 9 (Moon Sagittarius to Capricorn 3:52 a.m.)** The day starts out quite promisingly, and continues that way all the way through. You may even be shocked when someone extremely attractive of the opposite sex comes on very strong—and you didn't even know he/she noticed you. Enjoy the boost to your ego, and resolve not to start playing "control games" with this person.

**Friday, October 10 (Moon in Capricorn)** You and someone else could get into a face-off today—over something rather minor. Realize that you are feeling a little insecure and need to assert yourself. It could be the other person's problem too. Some Scorpios may find themselves taking off on an unexpected jaunt—maybe a combination of work and social life. Enjoy!

**Saturday, October 11 (Moon Capricorn to Aquarius 7:46 a.m.)** Delay a decision about money; this is one time when waiting will prove beneficial to your cause. Also try to become more open to new ideas; there will be a lot of them flying around you now. Someone in particular may challenge you, and you do not want to appear like a "dinosaur." Thinking young keeps you that way. The lucky number is 8.

**Sunday, October 12 (Moon in Aquarius)**　This day may be more exciting than you expect—or than you would like it to be. Don't make a fuss when you have to change plans rather quickly. You may be put out when a Leo dashes in and tries to grab the scene; give him/ her a run for the money by showing just how witty you can be when you try.

**Monday, October 13 (Moon Aquarius to Pisces 11:03 a.m.)**　You may not feel altogether like working today; the wanderlust may be upon you. Try to stick with the job at hand, letting your thoughts of pleasure stay in the back of your mind. That way, you will be ready for it when an impromptu invitation comes along. The lucky number is 1.

**Tuesday, October 14 (Moon in Pisces)**　You are generally one to stick by the rules (mainly because it makes you less conspicuous), However, today you will break one, and find that it gives you a lot more leeway. Today is a time to do what you wish, without too much guilt. You could find a lot of inspiration with a group of people who are really out for a good time.

**Wednesday, October 15 (Moon Pisces to Aries 5:13 p.m.)**　Today you could come crashing back to reality—and it could be a rather rude shock. There are things to be done and people depending on you; just do as much as you can. Get somebody to help you evaluate something—a situation or a person. Sometimes a second opinion is worth a lot.

**Thursday, October 16 (Moon in Aries)** Be bold about something today; there is no point in holding back your opinion, if it is a constructive one. You may be amazed and delighted when someone you work with turns out to have some similar interests; it's great to have a new "buddy." There may be an appointment you have to make in connection with your health.

**Friday, October 17 (Moon in Aries)** If you are not ready for it, this day could take you by surprise. The changes may come thick and fast, and you may have a number of opportunities to express yourself. Do it in a dynamic manner, because important people will be watching. Someone may try to steal your thunder, but that person really doesn't stand a chance.

**Saturday, October 18 (Moon Aries to Taurus 1:35 a.m.)** You should start out the weekend in a pretty mellow mood, and want nothing more than peace, quiet, and some time to goof off. However, someone could try to "disturb the peace," and you may have to change your plans. Be willing to go along with another opinion now; it really isn't time for you to force things.

*Sunday, October 19 (Moon in Taurus)*     Today you can expect someone to be very supportive of one of your "creative" ideas or projects; make sure you let him/her know how much you appreciate it. On the other hand, you are still going to have to face the fact that you can't call all the shots at this time. Be willing to take a back seat.

*Monday, October 20 (Moon Taurus to Gemini 12:15 p.m.)*     There is something you want today, but you can't quite put your finger on it. As you go along, you may better define your goals. Your desire to reach out for new things is quite strong now, and you should put it to good use. Some may find there is an opportunity to learn more about their field; grab it.

*Tuesday, October 21 (Moon in Gemini)*     Some confusion and resentment you have been feeling lately is totally put to rest when you get a message that someone really does care. Be sure to return it. In another scenario, Scorpios will find themselves having to deal with some tangled finances; if things don't clear up immediately, don't lose your patience. The lucky number is 9.

*Wednesday, October 22 (Moon in Gemini)*     The focus again today is on financial matters. Don't expect to make a fortune, but do use this time to make the most of your current assets. A rather talkative person is saying something—if you listen between the lines; there could be an important tip. A relationship is undergoing a rather drastic change.

146

*Thursday, October 23 (Moon Gemini to Cancer 12:37 a.m.)* The pieces of a puzzle are beginning to fall into place. Trust the conclusions you are arriving at how—as long as you have been properly analytical. Some rather conservative people are going to let you know how much they admire your style—and your stability. The lucky number is 2.

*Friday, October 24 (Moon in Cancer)* You may feel a little as if you are "all over the place" today; don't let it make you feel insecure. There are a lot of things to be done, and a lot of messages coming in, but you can handle it if you keep your cool. Some Scorpios may be thinking about furthering their education—or simply taking a course. Go to it.

*Saturday, October 25 (Moon Cancer to Leo 1:02 p.m.)* Today you recover your sense of standing on solid ground, and it may be through the help of someone who loves you very much. Later on, as you really pick up steam, you will want to go somewhere where you will be seen. It is possible someone may notice you in a very significant way, and it could lead to a valuable contact.

*Sunday, October 26 (Moon in Leo)* Get ready for a big change, and a possible encounter with someone rather aggressive. If you get into an argument, try to keep it on the light side; after all, there are no life-or-death issues involved. You don't always have to give your all to every situation you find yourself in; back off a bit. It's an excellent time to break out in something new. The lucky number is 5.

**Monday, October 27 (Moon Leo to Virgo 11:20 p.m.)**  You will discover who is a true friend today, as you find yourself grappling with a rather difficult problem. Someone will come through, and get you through it with flying colors. Enjoy the feeling of camaraderie it gives you, and plan a little celebration. No matter what the scenario, any Scorpio could be feeling rather generous today; just don't overextend yourself.

**Tuesday, October 28 (Moon in Virgo)**  Something you've been wishing and hoping for is now almost a reality; if you just stick with things a while longer, you will feel that wonderful sense of, "Yes, I really did it." Meanwhile, don't neglect some people who enjoy your company; they may ask you to "come out and play." Even if the time is not right, make sure you let them know you are still one of the crowd.

**Wednesday, October 29 (Moon in Virgo)**  You may have to adjust to the whims of others today, even if it is not particularly to your liking. Consider what someone tells you as "constructive criticism," and do not let it ruin your day. In fact, some Scorpios should listen carefully, because there are some practical suggestions you can put to use. The lucky number is 8.

**Thursday, October 30 (Moon Virgo to Libra 6:04 a.m.)**  You may welcome the chance to "crawl into a corner" today; for many, there will be quiet, unobtrusive work to do, but it will feel like a relief. This is one of those days many Scorpios will be feeling rather good-spirited and generous; don't waste the instincts. Make an openhearted gesture toward someone who needs it very badly.

**Friday, October 31 (Moon in Libra)**    Today you realize it is extremely difficult to go it alone; and how much your "significant other" means to you. Though you may not like to accept your dependency, accept the involvement—and take a responsible attitude toward it. Soon your rather wistful mood will dissipate, and you will feel more in control.

# NOVEMBER 1986

**Saturday, November 1 (Moon Libra to Scorpio 9:19 a.m.)**    Today you should feel ready to take on the world—and take charge of it as well. Just don't let it make you get too competitive; you can win the day without pushing others out of your way. You will be able to apply your excellent powers of perception to a rather murky situation—and seem absolutely clairvoyant. The lucky number is 8.

**Sunday, November 2 (Moon in Scorpio)**    Now it's time to dig in to a big project, and see just how much headway you can make. Though it is technically a day of rest, you will have too much energy to take too much time out. Be aware that a lot of eyes are on you, and be sure to look and act your best. You really do care, don't you?

**Monday, November 3 (Moon Scorpio to Sagittarius 10:19 a.m.)** — Regardless of your sex or your orientation, you are to have to make the first move in a romantic situation; in some cases, it may be a fascinating new person who suddenly appears. However, most Scorpios will be much more concerned about the amount of money funneling through their bank accounts; it may not be enough for your taste. Try some new methods.

**Tuesday, November 4 (Moon in Sagittarius)** You may be feeling a lot more experimental than usual; put the feeling to good use by seeing just how efficient you can make your current operation. As you streamline things, you will get a great sense of satisfaction. A Gemini could be a boon companion.

**Wednesday, November 5 (Moon Sagittarius to Capricorn 10:49 a.m.)** One sure-fire way to get the attention you want from a member of the opposite sex is to give in to the urge to buy those rather bold new clothes you've been eyeing lately. Face it; you are usually too conservative. Take some clues from a Cancer pal who really knows how to put it together and look great. The lucky number is 3.

**Thursday, November 6 (Moon in Capricorn)** Your attitude toward things today may be quite sober; in some cases, you may realize it is time to catch up on some family ties and "retie" them firmly. There is the possibility some will get the opportunity to play mentor to someone who really needs guidance. You should be good at the role.

**Friday, November 7 (Moon Capricorn to Aquarius 12:29 p.m.)**    You have a mission to accomplish today, and it may require taking a short side trip you didn't count on. In the course of it, you may run into some interesting new people who find you interesting too. Someone make a promise that is difficult to keep; don't hold him/her to it too strictly. The lucky number is 5.

**Saturday, November 8 (Moon in Aquarius)** Things are really going well now, and you could be feeling as if it's all downhill now. The problem is that there is a domestic problem to be solved, and only you can solve it. Be as unselfish as you can be—under the circumstances. And don't send someone on a guilt trip.

**Sunday, November 9 (Moon Aquarius to Pisces 4:30 p.m.)**    Today you can learn a valuable lesson from someone you respect; take it to heart. Not only will your relationship with this person grow stronger, but you'll benefit tremendously by his/her experience. Someone will also explain to you why he/she has been acting strangely lately; forgive it and forget it. The lucky number is 7.

**Monday, November 10 (Moon in Pisces)**    You could be in real danger of going over the edge today—in some kind of indulgence. In some cases, you could be "crazy with love," and willing to do anything for the object of your affection. Let logic have equal time with your emotions. Whatever you do today, do it with circumspection.

**Tuesday, November 11 (Moon Pisces to Aries 11:14 p.m.)**    Don't let someone pull the wool over your eyes today; you are still not in full control of your emotions. It's possible that there is some kind of intrigue going on where you work; avoid it at all costs. If you feel a little drained of energy, you should think about some "emergency" health measures.

**Wednesday, November 12 (Moon in Aries)**    You will deal with things a lot better today, if only because you've got more will to tackle problems. For some Scorpios, a health regime is in order, and they know it. For others, it's time to "take charge" of a work situation. Don't blow this opportunity. The lucky number is 1.

**Thursday, November 13 (Moon in Aries)**    You suddenly realize you were foolish to have the fears that have been plaguing you lately. When someone's views and intentions are clarified, you realize there was no reason for suspicion. Let it be a lesson to you. Any Scorpio should realize there are people standing behind you at this time, and there is plenty of support.

**Friday, November 14 (Moon Aries to Taurus 8:24 a.m.)**    You may decide it is the better part of valor to take on a task that is assigned to you today with grace—and a smile. The advice you've gotten confidentially tells you you are being put to some kind of test. You will prove you are up to it. Don't get involved in a "cat and mouse" game.

**Saturday, November 15 (Moon in Taurus)**    Today you may decide to get the facts on exactly what is expected of you. When you have them, you may decide that it is not worth the effort. In some cases, a marital or live-in arrangement may be coming to a close. Others will see "light at the end of the tunnel" when they realize a big responsibility is about to be taken off their shoulders.

**Sunday, November 16 (Moon Taurus to Gemini 7:26 p.m.)**    This full moon takes place right in the sector of your chart having to do with relationships; it may not be easy. However, it could also clear the air and make two people aware of what it really means to live as one. You could start out again on a whole new basis.

**Monday, November 17 (Moon in Gemini)**    You may have some rather shaky feelings about your finances today. In one sense, you are compelled to hang on to what you have; in another, you may feel the need to share your resources with someone else. Do not allow yourself to think of money as power; if you can have someone fair and square, there is no sense in trying to "buy" him/her.

**Tuesday, November 18 (Moon in Gemini)**    The emphasis today is on rather serious business, including the obligations that go along with new-found responsibility. Though you must concentrate on something rather intensely for part of the day, you should be able to steal some "talking time" to

153

interact with someone rather lively. Another Scorpio might be just the ticket today.

***Wednesday, November 19 (Moon Gemini to Cancer 7:46 a.m.)***     Refuse to be distracted from the work at hand today; your interests could easily be fragmented by some unexpected developments. However, you can expect a nod of approval for a job well done, and you should feel a warm glow at being recognized. It was all worth it, wasn't it?

***Thursday, November 20 (Moon in Cancer)*** Some irrational feelings of jealousy could intrude on your thoughts today; try to be logical and rational about a situation that seems to be something that it is not. You are never sure of someone's loyalty to you; realize that is the reason you are experiencing problems with him/ her. The lucky number today is 9.

***Friday, November 21 (Moon Cancer to Leo 8:25 p.m.)***     Your urge for power could rise to the surface today and be the impetus to take a bold step. As you go straight to the point, you may realize how easy it is to get what you want when you assert yourself. Also realize that there is a vast difference between being assertive—and aggressive. Hostility never got anyone anywhere.

***Saturday, November 22 (Moon in Leo)***     You could be so full of get-up-and-go today that you are frustrated about having a challenging outlet for your energy. Try getting involved in an activity where you can lead—and be recognized for your leadership ability. For many Scorpios the opportunity will appear in the form of a community group that means well—but doesn't know how to get started. Show them.

**Sunday, November 23 (Moon in Leo)**    It may become obvious to you today that you have been neglecting some important people in your circle—possibly young people. And, that you have been depriving yourself of pleasure in the process. To right things, get a group together and let them play "follow the leader." Everyone will enjoy it—including you.

**Monday, November 24 (Moon Leo to Virgo 7:46 a.m.)**    Your hopes and dreams seem so close you should be able to touch them, but the time has not come yet. Since you are a bit frustrated, you may seek solace in finding fault with others; that won't help anyone, least of all you. Let a sensitive Pisces show you how to relax.

**Tuesday, November 25 (Moon in Virgo)**    Could be a beautiful day during which someone responds to you in exactly the way you hoped. Do not spoil the romantic atmosphere by nit-picking about things that don't count at all in the long run. Some Scorpios may be tempted to go off on a tangent; just be sure you keep your eye on what is most important to accomplish now. The lucky number is 5.

**Wednesday, November 26 (Moon Virgo to Libra 3:59 p.m.)**    Some friends may ask you to join the party; do it and have fun. Your sense of humor should be rather keen, and you should be feeling rather sociable—particularly for you. The hectic pace of recent days may tempt you to relax too far; you can indulge yourself without going completely overboard. You will make an excellent impression on someone.

**Thursday, November 27 (Moon in Libra)**     No matter what happens today, just smile and say "You are right." This is no time to get tough with anyone. Least of all yourself. In fact, you Scorpios would do well to give yourselves a break now; you have been driving rather hard of late. In your mood, the best thing would be some sweet music— and company to match.

**Friday, November 28 (Moon Libra to Scorpio 8:13 p.m.)**     You will feel as if everything is "on hold" today; nothing seems to be moving forward. If it makes you feel restricted, try to get your mind on comforting things like the joyful season coming up. Have you started thinking about how you are going to let those you love know how much you love them?

**Saturday, November 29 (Moon in Scorpio)**     You should feel your vitality returning now, and you should feel your spirits soaring with it. Now you should be able to make that impressive move, and "knock the socks off" someone you've been wanting to impress. Some Scorpios should take care not to get overbearing with those around them now; remember, there is more than one way to do things than your way. The lucky number is 9.

**Sunday, November 30 (Moon Scorpio to Sagittarius 9:08 p.m.)** Finances can sometimes take over and color everything else for you; this could be one of those days. Try to rise above your doubts and fears about being able to make it and concentrate on the larger picture. There is more to life than this! An enterprising person may come on the scene and get you out of your rut. Good for him/her!

# DECEMBER 1986

**Monday, December 1 (Moon in Sagittarius)** Today you will get a warm glow when someone who has seemed rather indifferent lately comes to you and not only wants to make up—but also wants to confide and to ask your advice. Be willing to forget the past and do what you can to help. Even if you are tempted, don't start giving any lectures. You need this opening-up experience.

**Tuesday, December 2 (Moon Sagittarius to Capricorn 8:26 p.m.)** Now you realize that your money situation is more flexible than you thought, and you feel more comfortable with whatever your assets happen to be at the moment. However, don't relax too far, because you are still going to have to keep a close watch on things. Later on, you will be called upon to play "teacher" to someone who's gotten into a mess. Be kind and wise as you can.

### Wednesday, December 3 (Moon in Capricorn)

You may find yourself cast in the role of "the sensible one" as people around you seem to be "losing it." Keep cool and keep everyone together. Some Scorpios will find that there is a lot of unanticipated activity—a lot of it involving messages coming in. Don't get too rigid about plans that have been made; they can always be changed.

### Thursday, December 4 (Moon Capricorn to Aquarius 8:23 p.m.)

You are in everyone's good graces today as you display your marvelous sense of humor and bring everyone together for some fun. Your family ties will be strengthened, and you will enjoy the opportunity to socialize. You may find a rather formidable adversary in a "battle of wits"; don't take it too seriously.

### Friday, December 5 (Moon in Aquarius)

At this time of the year, you are feeling more and more home-and family-oriented; today that sense is stronger than ever. You may be a bit concerned about security matters, but just don't become overly concerned. You are a worrier by nature, and your feelings now could be exaggerated. Try your luck with number 4 today.

### Saturday, December 6 (Moon Aquarius to Pisces 10:48 p.m.)

This could be a day of rather mixed emotions. You are a bit annoyed with someone who seems to be "putting you to the test," but you also are able to score some points by proving that you know how to do your homework—and change your ways. In some cases, an estrangement is healing, and you are beginning to form a new and better relationship. It is a good feeling.

**Sunday, December 7 (Moon in Pisces)**   The holiday spirit could descend on you with a vengeance today, and you could go out on a spending spree. Hang on to your dollars and your sense as well; there are ways of showing your love and admiration for people without totally wrecking your bank account. Some will find themselves involved in joint ventures with people as carried away with the holidays as they are; try to keep each other on the track.

**Monday, December 8 (Moon in Pisces)**   This is definitely not a halfway day. There is intensity in the atmosphere, and those around you may be rather demanding—particularly in the emotional area. Try to cool things off, and to carry out your own duties with good will and good grace. This is no day to tangle with people in high places. The lucky number is 7.

**Tuesday, December 9 (Moon Pisces to Aries 4:40 a.m.)**   It will be a lot easier for you to dig in and get your day-to-day chores knocked off in record time. Your energy level should be very high. However, you could get a little high-handed with people around you; remember that yours is not the only method of doing things. Curb an impulse to speak very sharply—to anyone.

**Wednesday, December 10 (Moon in Aries)**   Now you should be able to take the lead—no matter what circle you find yourself moving in today.

You could get an important offer from someone today, and you should be able to look at it with a critical and discriminating eye. However, you are wise to put off taking definite action until all the facts of the case are in. It won't be long.

**Thursday, December 11 (Moon Aries to Taurus 2:10 p.m.)**   There is something extremely important that you must get across today, and you realize you've got to handle it with a lot of seriousness. This is no time to exhibit a casual attitude. Since your mind is sharp, you should be able to get your message across with conviction. In some cases, a serious commitment is about to be made.

**Friday, December 12 (Moon in Taurus)**   Today it is time to back down, and to let someone else score points; you have "had your day," at least for the moment. Your mood should be mellow, and you should be able to take a back seat with grace. This is one of those times you can make your presence and love felt most strongly by doing something that everyone can appreciate. Why not try buying a real luxury that will make you look like a hero?

**Saturday, December 13 (Moon in Taurus)**   Today should be a very productive one; you can pull out all the stops and do what needs to be done very effectively. However, you may still not feel as if you are in total control; it is not the time for that. Accept the role you must play with another now. Some Scorpios will be coming in contact with someone who seems soft and pliant; don't be deceived by appearances. The lucky number is 3 today.

*Sunday, December 14 (Moon Taurus to Gemini 1:41 a.m.)*     In spite of the approaching holiday, you and someone else could easily square off today—and the bone of contention could be joint finances. Try not to let things get out of hand, and try to keep an open mind. It is one time you should concentrate on opening up and exchanging ideas instead of sticking rigidly to your own. Stay loose!

*Monday, December 15 (Moon in Gemini)*     You could be exceptionally well equipped today to put a pet idea across—especially one that has to do with making a good thing better. It is a time to exhibit versatility, and a willingness to communicate ideas in an open manner. For best results, team up with a Sagittarian who knows how to handle "big deals."

*Tuesday, December 16 (Moon Gemini to Cancer 2:09 p.m.)*     You may have been underestimating your potential recently; someone could make that clear to you today when he/she says, "you're terrific." Though the exact words may be different, the message will be clear. Some security needs may seem to overwhelm you now, but you can make it all better by spending some intimate time with those who obviously care about you. The lucky number is 6.

*Wednesday, December 17 (Moon in Cancer)*     If you can, take some time out to retreat with the purpose of "recharging." If your nerves seem a bit frazzled, put your mind on things that are less immediate; this is one time the world could be "too much with you." Some Scorpios may even be thinking about a drastic change in life or career direction. Keep on thinking, but don't make any rash moves.

**Thursday, December 18 (Moon in Cancer)**  It's time to evaluate some business opportunities in new areas; you may find you need further training or education to get just what you want. If you show how serious you are to someone in authority, you will get the backing you need—both emotional and financial.

**Friday, December 19 (Moon Cancer to Leo 2:44 a.m.)**  Complete an important project at work and then step back and see where you stand. You might find that it is in a very good place. Talk to people who are pioneers in their field and have progressive ideas about the future. Don't let the holiday season distract you. Your lucky number today is 9.

**Saturday, December 20 (Moon in Leo)**  Your prestige will increase through the company you keep. You'll bask in the reflected glory of someone else who is the center of attention wherever you go. Though this person is a showoff, he/she definitely needs your approval. Be sensitive to that fact.

**Sunday, December 21 (Moon Leo to Virgo 2:30 p.m.)**  A parent or parent figure is rooting for you, in spite of how gruff he/she seems today. The accent is on your reputation and you should concentrate on getting yourself extra prestige. You can be sure of the emotional support of people around you now. And you will be feeling in need of reassurance. Your lucky number is 2.

**Monday, December 22 (Moon in Virgo)** Your social life expands to fill up every available minute. Don't schedule more than you can handle however. A visitor from a distance—or at least some new personality—comes on the scene and dazzles you. Learn all you can from this person.

**Tuesday, December 23 (Moon in Virgo)** One of your fondest wishes can come true if you see a project through to the bitter end. You may have to forego some social events now and concentrate on the nitty-gritty of practical preparations for the festivities ahead. An Aquarian or a Leo could figure prominently.

**Wednesday, December 24 (Moon Virgo to Libra 12:05 a.m.)** There is definitely a lot of activity on the agenda; however, you will hear a secret that may be tempted to tell. It is important to keep your lips sealed so some fun is not spoiled for someone else. Be ready for surprises and changes of plan. Your lucky number is 5.

**Thursday, December 25 (Moon in Libra)** A quiet family-oriented holiday is on the calendar. You will want to enjoy as many private moments as possible only with those you truly love and enjoy. A slight disagreement can be settled behind the scenes and not disturb anyone's fun. Keep an eye on a Taurus.

*Friday, December 26 (Moon Libra to Scorpio 7:06 a.m.)* You may seem a bit remote to those around you, but that's because you're tuned into that "still small voice" within you. The accent today is definitely on your spiritual values and dreams. Stay part of the crowd and realize that you can be "in it" and "out of it" at the same time. Your lucky number is 7.

*Saturday, December 27 (Moon in Scorpio)* Today you definitely step back into the real world and should be able to take a leadership position. For many Scorpios this could be a very significant day, and one in which past efforts pay off. All limits are off, and you can make definite headway in any or all areas of your life. Advice from a Capricorn can help considerably.

*Sunday, December 28 (Moon Scorpio to Sagittarius 8:20 a.m.)* You may be moved to be quite charitable today. You are right to be generous with those less fortunate than yourself. In some cases, it won't be money that Scorpio invests, but time and emotion. An Aries or a Libra can be an excellent person to team up with today. The lucky number today is 9.

*Monday, December 29 (Moon in Sagittarius)* An original approach can pay off now. Many Scorpios will be making a new start in a new direction, and may be offered the opportunity to get in on the ground floor. Someone who is willing to share some trade secrets with you is doing you a big favor—if you will only recognize it. It may require an investment of some sort.

*Tuesday, December 30 (Moon Sagittarius to Capricorn 7:54 a.m.)* If you give in to your emotions today, you could easily stray off the course. Use your time to gather facts and figures, but do not force any issues now. Someone may call you on your tendency to change your opinion on a moment's notice; you could get a reputation for being rather fickle. Simply relax and go with the flow.

*Wednesday, December 31 (Moon in Capricorn)* This New Year's Eve could find you far from home—among fascinating new people. Even if your particular scenario does not include travel, some kind of "adventure" will come into your life now. If you handle it right, it could be the key to starting out the New Year on a brilliant note.


# JANUARY 1987


*Thursday, January 1 (Moon Capricorn to Aquarius 6:53 a.m.)* Your true Scorpio power emerges, but in a responsible, sensible manner. Relationships intensify, and commitments are made. Home and family are accented; your ambition to provide for loved ones is strongly stimulated. Your lucky number is 8.

**Friday, January 2 (Moon in Aquarius)**  A powerful new year is getting under way—don't cling to the past. See beyond the current limitations of your living quarters; expansion of space will be possible soon. Security needs *will* be provided for if you have faith. An Aries is in the picture.

**Saturday, January 3 (Moon Aquarius to Pisces 7:36 a.m.)**  Your personal magnetism surges to a high point, bringing new possibilities where romance is concerned. Break free from your home chores and seek exciting entertainment, recreation, or creative activity. One who is proud, dramatic, and loving plays a key role.

**Sunday, January 4 (Moon in Pisces)**  Your contentment is right in your own backyard, so to speak. Your whimsical moods and sense of humor will appeal to a younger family member—you can get much mileage out of your creative imagination. An older woman provides a feeling of being needed.

**Monday, January 5 (Moon Pisces to Aries 11:51 a.m.)**  The accent is on travel, social events, and intellectual curiosity about new findings in work and health. Ask questions that are on your mind; you'll find others receptive to an exchange of ideas. Sagittarius and Gemini people figure prominently. Your lucky number is 3.

**Tuesday, January 6 (Moon in Aries)**  Routine matters prevail; you'll feel most comfortable sticking to small details and letting someone else make the major decisions. You'll accomplish much through diligent attention to duty. Rewards are on the way. Aquarius and Leo are involved.

**Wednesday, January 7 (Moon Aries to Taurus 8:13 p.m.)**   Make allowances for your romantic partner or co-workers today. A flexible point of view will be needed to deal with many changes and alterations from the original plans. A love affair takes surprise direction—go with the flow. Your lucky number is 5.

**Thursday, January 8 (Moon in Taurus)**   The concerns and problems of others dominate your day. Your tactful ability to smoothe over disagreements will create greater domestic harmony. Treat your partner to a luxury dinner or entertainment in a warm, affectionate manner. Libra is on your side.

**Friday, January 9 (Moon in Taurus)**   Learn the inside story before you make demands on your partner, mate, or associate. You're likely to fall in love with love or deceive yourself where love and partnership are concerned. Pisces and Virgo people are featured today. Your lucky number is 7.

**Saturday, January 10 (Moon Taurus to Gemini 7:39 a.m.)**   A romantic relationship intensifies, leading to greater commitments, especially involving joint finances and resources. You'll seek depth, permanence, and sincerity in an affair of the heart. A psychic bond between you and your loved one is forged.

*Sunday, January 11 (Moon in Gemini)*    A larger view of life helps you expand and transform your views in a positive, upbeat manner. Generosity to those in need will be highlighted, but draw the line at merely being used. A person with futuristic, humanitarian ideals plays an important role in the scenario.

*Monday, January 12 (Moon Gemini to Cancer 8:18 p.m.)*    You make a new start involving money, travel, and further job training. Original methods succeed; listen to the voice of intuition and break free of old formulas. A fascinating stranger enters the picture and shows romantic inclinations. Your lucky number is 1.

*Tuesday, January 13 (Moon in Cancer)*    You'll borrow your life-style and philosophy from the past, turning to more conventional ideas and habits. Communication from a family member at a distance turns the tide of events; a downcast mood can surge to one of elation. Your security needs will be met!

*Wednesday, January 14 (Full Moon in Cancer)* The full moon highlights travel, expansion of plans, and optimistic views about the future. Parties and social events throw you in the company of lively intellectual types who may oppose your own ideas, but in a good-humored, lighthearted manner.

*Thursday, January 15 (Moon Cancer to Leo 8:45 a.m.)*    Review and revise your career plans; possibly additional training is needed. Investigate seminars and study groups and build a solid foundation for the future. You'll have the ability to stick to a job until it's done. Aquarius inspires you. Lucky number is 4.

**Friday, January 16 (Moon in Leo)**    Your career plans surge forward because of a well-written request or memo. Don't hesitate to present original ideas to one in authority—this is the time for a real meeting of minds. A romantic partner encourages you to get ahead. Your lucky number is 5.

**Saturday, January 17 (Moon Leo to Virgo 8:15 p.m.)**    Musical, artistic, and decorative skills help you gain the recognition you deserve. A family member may be one to push you forward into the limelight and insist you be noticed. A glamorous social event enlivens the evening hours, possibly at your own home.

**Sunday, January 18 (Moon in Virgo)**    Your wishes and desires may verge on the unrealistic. You'll be inspired by a friend or associate with highly spiritual aspirations to reach beyond ordinary levels of accomplishment. A few select friends make the best company today, especially a Pisces person.

**Monday, January 19 (Moon in Virgo)**    Clubs, groups, and organizations grant you recognition for past efforts. You'll naturally assume a leadership role that puts you in a prestigious position. Stop merely talking about important goals; take serious steps to achieve them. Your lucky number is 8.

**Tuesday, January 20 (Moon Virgo to Libra 6:09 a.m.)**   You'll have the opportunity to display the real humanitarian side of your personality in dealings with those less fortunate than yourself. Don't hide your light under a bushel; show your talents to those with progressive attitudes. Petty limitations have no place in your life.

**Wednesday, January 21 (Moon in Libra)**   Secret backing arrives for original ideas and concepts. It's not yet time to reveal your ideas to the general public, but one with warmth, generosity, and a fiery manner becomes your avid promoter. Spend some time alone to develop your blossoming talents.

**Thursday, January 22 (Moon Libra to Scorpio 1:30 p.m.)**   Your keen intuition will help you sense upsurge in personal power as the day progresses. You'll be in the driver's seat, but may need to temper your personality plays and moods with a note of diplomacy. Be sensitive to the feelings of others. Your lucky number is 2.

**Friday, January 23 (Moon in Scorpio)**   You'll be extra aware of your body image and fashions. The strong lunar cycle helps you present yourself in the best light, making you more popular than ever. You'll attract those with ideas and theories to discuss. Maintain a light touch and a sense of humor.

**Saturday, January 24 (Moon Scorpio to Sagittarius 5:35 p.m.)**   Attend to your health needs early in the day, checking on vitamins, nutrition, and a general state of well-being. Later a shopping trip helps you obtain the necessities of everyday life. Stick to routine tasks and practical projects. Your lucky number is 4.

**Sunday, January 25 (Moon in Sagittarius)**
You'll have some new moneymaking ideas and know how to put them into action. An exciting change of pace frees you from boring tasks and brings a generous lover into the picture. A heart-to-heart talk about mutual values will pay off well.

**Monday, January 26 (Moon Sagittarius to Capricorn 6:42 p.m.)**     Your local neighborhood is the scene of a special celebration or get-together among friends and relatives. You'll spend lavishly to provide a lovely background and gourmet dining. A conversation about a change of location becomes a key topic. Your lucky number is 6.

**Tuesday, January 27 (Moon in Capricorn)**
You'll dwell on a higher plane of inspiration and idealism—or you could escape into a self-pitying scenario if you fail to count your blessings. Avoid signing contracts or making definite commiments until you've come back down to earth. A Pisces is up there with you.

**Wednesday, January 28 (Moon Capricorn to Aquarius 6:17 p.m.)**     A parent or parent figure is on your side and will back you in an ambitious project, if you communicate a responsible atti-tude. Real estate, domestic products, and work in the home is favored. Your business sense is highly reliable; depend on it! Your lucky number is 8.

*Thursday, January 29 (Moon in Aquarius)* The new moon accents new projects and endeavors that benefit large groups of people. You'll do better by expanding your views optimistically than clinging to petty matters from the past. Pioneering types will encourage you to reassess your values and make a new start.

*Friday, January 30 (Moon Aquarius to Pisces 6:24 p.m.)* A romantic lover pursues you with pleasure in mind. You'll exude sex appeal and charisma and act as a magnet for members of the opposite sex. Creative abilities are at a high point; develop original ideas and express yourself dramatically. Your lucky number is 1.

*Saturday, January 31 (Moon in Pisces)* A domestic drama takes center stage. Family members flock around you, responding to your warm manner and taste for entertaining activities. Provide comfort, good food, and reassurance, but don't force your own ideas on impressionable younger minds.

# FEBRUARY 1987

*Sunday, February 1 (Moon Pisces to Aries 9:09 p.m.)* The successful resolution to affair of the heart depends upon taking a broader viewpoint and paying greater attention to long-range plans.

Petty jealousy should have no place in your relationship. Someone with futuristic ideas figures prominently. Your lucky number is 9.

**Monday, February 2 (Moon in Aries)**   A new method of promoting creative talents puts you in the spotlight at your scene of employment. You'll have an innovative idea for accomplishing tasks more efficiently and will have reason to be proud of the results. Leo and Aquarius people are impressed.

**Tuesday, February 3 (Moon in Aries)**   Catch up on personal concerns, including health and nutrition programs. The focus will be on food, security, and family well-being. A natural tendency will be to give advice for another's own good. Don't force issues in doing so. Be diplomatic.

**Wednesday, February 4 (Moon Aries to Taurus 8:53 a.m.)**   Your social life expands as you contact people from different areas and backgrounds than your own. You'll be asked to go along with the plans of others, including your partner, mate, or associate. Maintain a sense of humor. Your lucky number is 3.

**Thursday, February 5 (Moon in Taurus)**   Avoid extremes in dealing with legalities and public relations. You'll do better to play the waiting game than insist on your rights. Check the fine print of a contract, making sure you haven't overlooked an important detail. Stick to routine duties.

*Friday, February 6 (Moon Taurus to Gemini 2:23 p.m.)* A member of the opposite sex has serious intentions, possibly leading to an alliance. Listen closely to what is said; then be ready to change your plans at moment's notice. You'll hear words you've been waiting for. Gemini and Virgo play key roles.

*Saturday, February 7 (Moon in Gemini)* Romantic success depends on tact, graciousness, and an appeal to the sentimental nature of your loved one. Flowers, gifts, gourmet dining, and a special atmosphere can create the mood you desire. Don't neglect your own appearance. Your lucky number is 6.

*Sunday, February 8 (Moon in Gemini)* Dig deep for answers regarding a puzzling relationship; you'll hear secrets if you show compassion for another. Draw the line, however, at making loans or co-signing for one who has not previously shown responsibility where money is concerned.

*Monday, February 9 (Moon Gemini to Cancer 2:55 a.m.)* Higher education, a legal matter, or faraway places could be the key to greater commercial success. An enterprising spirit will help you gain in career and prestige and could win you the financial backing you need. Put your plans into action. Your lucky number is 8.

*Tuesday, February 10 (Moon in Cancer)* The emphasis is on successful completion of a long-range project. You'll gain wider appeal through taking a universal viewpoint. A trip to an art gallery, concert, or other cultural event is a good idea. Aries and Libra are interested.

**Wednesday, February 11 (Moon Cancer to Leo 3:21 p.m.)**    A fascinating stranger will be met on travels or in your professional capacity. Wear bold colors so that you stand out in a crowd; you have much to offer in both love and career, but need to call special attention to yourself. A Leo person plays a key role.

**Thursday, February 12 (Moon in Leo)** Emotions come to the surface and there's a call for a decision between personal and public duties. Pay attention to your family needs and security in spite of added pressure from top executives. Patience and diplomacy help you deal successfully with vital issues.

**Friday, February 13 (Full Moon in Leo)**    You'll benefit professionally from your social contacts, journeys, classes, or seminars that increase your scope of knowledge during this full moon. So many opportunities suddenly arise that you may have difficulty choosing the best course; don't scatter your forces. Your lucky number is 3.

**Saturday, February 14 (Moon Leo to Virgo 2:26 a.m.)**    Show the community that you are a solid citizen by attending to duties rather than rushing off to a social event. An Aquarius friend presents a special temptation to cut corners and escape from the mass of details. This will be a testing time—work and wait.

**Sunday, February 15 (Moon in Virgo)**    A romantic wish comes true through opening lines of communication with one who is lively, active, and mentally stimulating. A social event in your local neighborhood may be the scene of an exciting development. Be ready for change, variety. Your lucky number is 5.

**Monday, February 16 (Moon Virgo to Libra 11:44 a.m.)**    You'll be asked to listen to the problems of a friend or acquaintance, and can help through keeping a cheerful attitude and a diplomatic manner. Keep confidences that are revealed in a behind-the-scenes chat later in the day. Libra, Taurus, and another Scorpio are involved.

**Tuesday, February 17 (Moon in Libra)**    A retreat from activities will give you chance to rest and relax, tune into spiritual values, and get closer to nature—especially your own. You'll soon be in a position to translate the inspirations you received into practical projects.

**Wednesday, February 18 (Moon Libra to Scorpio 7:05 p.m.)**    The moon enters your own sign during the day, placing the focus on you, your personality, and your ability to call the shots. Leadership of a responsible nature is indicated, along with a gain in prestige and intensification of romance. Your lucky number is 8.

**Thursday, February 19 (Moon in Scorpio)**
Greater personal self-expression is on the agenda. Broaden your horizons and focus on the big picture. Artistic or altruistic tendencies will be espe-

cially favored, and a fuller potential of talents will be shown. Aries and Libra people come into focus.

**Friday, February 20 (Moon in Scorpio)**    You'll dance to your own tune with independence, originality, and a flair for the dramatic. Your romantic partners are drawn by your magnetism, charisma, and daring approach to life. Don't be afraid to blow your own horn. Your lucky number is 1.

**Saturday, February 21 (Moon Scorpio to Sagittarius 12:09 a.m.)**    The accent is on security, savings accounts, and assurance of love and affection. You'll be drawn to a domestic scene, replete with good food, recreation, and creature comforts. Children and young people play vital roles in a highly emotional drama.

**Sunday, February 22 (Moon in Sagittarius)**    A versatile, lighthearted attitude to a communication project will pay off in monetary gain. You'll say what you think, but people will find you amusing, entertaining, and intellectually stimulating. Sagittarius and Gemini are on your side.

**Monday, February 23 (Moon Sagittarius to Capricorn 2:57 a.m.)**    This day of routine involves you in the details of messages, letters, telephone calls, and spreading the word efficiently. Build foundations now for the future by reviewing, revising, and rebuilding, if necessary, on a more solid basis. Your lucky number is 4.

**Tuesday, February 24 (Moon in Capricorn)**
Exciting developments in your local neighborhood revolve around romance, questions and answers, and creative thinking. You'll learn the complete story about a fascinating member of the opposite sex, leading to a dramatic change of heart. A Gemini gets your attention.

**Wednesday, February 25 (Moon Capricorn to Aquarius 9:08 a.m.)** Beautify your surroundings and prepare for a family celebration. Sentiment and romance figure prominently in happenings on the home front. You'll have an excellent chance to upgrade your living conditions through a diplomatic approach. Your lucky number is 6.

**Thursday, February 26 (Moon in Aquarius)**
Your home becomes your refuge as you escape from the hustle and bustle of current events. Take advantage of a period of confinement to improve your basic skills and talents and to seek inspiration from the beauties of nature. Pisces and Virgo people share your feelings.

**Friday, February 27 (Moon Aquarius to Pisces 5:07 a.m.)** The new moon accents romantic and creative opportunities, including an intensification of an existing love relationship. If single, you'll attract marriage. If already married, you'll talk about a vital addition to the family. Your lucky number is 8.

**Saturday, February 28 (Moon in Pisces)** Complete a creative project so that you can seek new fields to conquer. You'll be operating at your full potential if you release petty problems that stifle your imagination. Associate with people who are pioneers and self-starters at a glamorous entertainment event.

# MARCH 1987

**Sunday, March 1 (Moon Pisces to Aries 7:37 a.m.)** A new you emerges, ready for romance, changes in your appearance, and exciting entertainment plans. Renewed vitality will help you deal with extra chores that come up later in the day. Be bold in your expression of affections. Your lucky number is 1.

**Monday, March 2 (Moon in Aries)** Cooperation is the key to success in a work project today. You'll be willing to follow another's lead, especially where home and security are involved. Emotional needs might lead to overeating; watch your diet and don't push yourself. An older woman has good advice.

**Tuesday, March 3 (Moon Aries to Taurus 1:11 p.m.)** You'll work well with co-workers or the public, spreading optimism and good humor. A whirlwind of activity will include socializing, parties, and an exchange of witty stories. Don't overestimate your energies; let another share the load, especially details.

**Wednesday, March 4 (Moon in Taurus)**    A marital or business partner or associate is counting on you for solid assistance in routine duties. A relationship will be tested by your ability to stick to a task, overcome obstacles, and see a project through. Your lucky number is 4.

**Thursday, March 5 (Moon Taurus to Gemini 10:26 p.m.)**    Today brings change, travel, variety, and communication with an exciting member of opposite sex. A mercurial type of person expects you to alter your plans at moment's notice. Be ready for questions and ánswers and a transformation of rigid views.

**Friday, March 6 (Moon in Gemini)**    Make adjustments in family spending—a few luxury items could spell the difference between harmony and unhappiness. A special occasion or anniversary should be observed in beautiful style. Libra, Taurus, and another Scorpio celebrate with you.

**Saturday, March 7 (Moon in Gemini)**    Play the waiting game where borrowing, lending, or making investments are concerned. The current financial picture is fuzzy and needs clearing up before you commit yourself to a long-term obligation. Dig deep for information. Your lucky number is 7.

**Sunday, March 8 (Moon Gemini to Cancer 10:24 a.m.)**    The emphasis is on business, responsibilities, and a gain in prestige. Nothing occurs halfway; you'll associate with the top people in your field and can gain favors from an authority figure. Joint financial concerns are favored. A Capricorn is on your side.

**Monday, March 9 (Moon in Cancer)**     Opportunities multiply as you expand views and contacts, and look to the future for inspiration. Travel, publishing, and higher education are good possibilities to consider. Release petty concerns and persons from your life. Your lucky number is 9.

**Tuesday, March 10 (Moon Cancer to Leo 10:54 p.m.)**     Focus on new ideas, philosophies, and boldness to exhibit a more individualistic life-style. Someone from afar arrives to bolster self-confidence and show you off in an entertaining round of events. Wear distinctive clothing; stand out in the crowd!

**Wednesday, March 11 (Moon in Leo)**     A family member proves to be valuable contact in dealing with your career, advancement or authority figures. Be patient; hang onto your present security rather than risking all in a bold move today. Cancer and Capricorn persons are supportive.

**Thursday, March 12 (Moon in Leo)**     You'll be optimistic, talkative, and ready to share information to others. You have all the answers today. You'll be extra aware of your body image; dress for success and groom yourself carefully. Your popularity is assured. Your lucky number is 3.

**Friday, March 13 (Moon Leo to Virgo 9:55 a.m.)**  The rewards of past endeavors begin to show up, but caution is advised. Pay attention to details, apply the finishing touches, and see the project through to completion. You'll be tempted to break away from the task in order to socialize or escape the routine.

**Saturday, March 14 (Moon in Virgo)**    A romantic message arrives, leading to change in plans and exciting developments. Make personal wishes known and expect a change of scenery, brief trips, and fulfilling social events. A talkative person with bright, new ideas is on the scene.

**Sunday, March 15 (Full Moon in Virgo to Libra 6 p.m.)**    The full moon coincides with family disagreements over entertainment plans. You'll win through a tactful manner and subtle manipulation rather than blunt statement of wishes. Beautify your surroundings and create harmony around you. Your lucky number is 6.

**Monday, March 16 (Moon in Libra)**    Be aware of hidden clues and follow instincts; do not tell all you know. Get the real story before you proceed. You'll discover inner springs of inspiration through a brief period of contemplation in private. Watch a Pisces.

**Tuesday, March 17 (Moon in Libra)**    Negotiations behind the scenes will lead to a more powerful position. One in a role of authority is willing to listen to the facts and figures, and admires the progress you have already made in a large-scale endeavor. You're on the way up! Your lucky number is 8.

**Wednesday, March 18 (Moon Libra to Scorpio 12:57 a.m.)**    Put aside petty personal plans in order to help with a large project that will help many throughout the world. You'll have the talents to win others over to your cause and can influence also through artistic or literary skills. A pioneer type is in the picture.

**Thursday, March 19 (Moon in Scorpio)**    The high lunar cycle puts you in the driver's seat, ready to make a bold splash in the world. Wear the latest styles and take advantage of renewed vitality to promote your personal plans. A romantic, dynamic member of the opposite sex will respond. Your lucky number is 1.

**Friday, March 20 (Moon Scorpio to Sagittarius 5:32 a.m.)**    Don't brood over past errors or mistakes where cash in concerned; merely resolve to spend more carefully in the future. Your sense of security will be highlighted, pushing you to make a budget and concentrate on saving for that rainy day. Don't force the issues now.

**Saturday, March 21 (Moon in Sagittarius)**    The social whirl leads you to concentrate on your wardrobe and wish to update many items. Remember yesterday's resolve about spending—devise clever ways to make the most of what you already possess. Sagittarius and Gemini people are communicative.

**Sunday, March 22 (Moon Sagittarius to Capricorn 8:48 a.m.)**    You'll have an excellent chance to catch up on the details of record-keeping, correspondence, and other personal business. Don't allow a gabby relative or pal to distract you from your duties. You'll feel a solid glow of accomplishment at the day's end. Your lucky number is 4.

**Monday, March 23 (Moon in Capricorn)**  A fast-talking neighbor or associate could transform your views. Be open to new ideas and creative thinking. A romantic relationship blossoms if you communicate affectionate feelings—don't clam up now. Gemini and Virgo people have much to say today.

**Tuesday, March 24 (Moon Capricorn to Aquarius 11:18 a.m.)**  A family gathering is on the agenda. You'll rediscover loved ones, receive a special gift, and enjoy beautified surroundings. A disturbing influence in your home will be removed if you use tact and patience. Don't overindulge your "sweet tooth." Your lucky number is 6.

**Wednesday, March 25 (Moon in Aquarius)** Your personal feelings of security depend on assessing spiritual values and determining to be more true to your own objectives. An older person or family member acts as a confidant in a revealing discussion. Don't give way to destructive methods of escape.

**Thursday, March 26 (Moon Aquarius to Pisces 1:46 p.m.)**  A serious romantic relationship becomes the topic of a family discussion. You'll have eyes on long-term commitments rather than shallow romantic opportunities. Creative projects are favored, leading to greater prestige in the near future. Your lucky number is 8.

**Friday, March 27 (Moon in Pisces)**     You won't be satisfied with the same old types of entertainment; your eye is on the future and big projects, worldwide views. You'll have a chance to meet people who are pioneers, healers, artists, and altruists. You can make the right decision today!

**Saturday, March 28 (Moon Pisces to Aries 5 p.m.)** Your personal magnetism and charisma are high— you'll attract a prestigious member of opposite sex who exudes warmth and caring. Take the lead in making new contacts at a social occasion; now is the time to blow your own horn. Your lucky number is 1.

**Sunday, March 29 (Moon in Aries)**     The new moon highlights health, employment, pets, and dependents. Don't allow others to take advantage of your desire to please; now is not the time to take on extra duties. Seek a relaxing atmosphere, surrounded by those you love and admire.

**Monday, March 30 (Moon Aries to Taurus 10:46 p.m.)**     Your sense of humor and optimistic self-expression wins you favor with daily associates. You'll work better with big ideas rather than small details, however. Teaching, writing, traveling, and socializing are favored. Your lucky number is 3.

**Tuesday, March 31 (Moon in Taurus)**     The accent is on partnerships, legalities, marital status, and improved public image. A practical manner helps you relate better to those who can grant favors; prove yourself by seeing a project through to completion. An Aquarius supports you.

# APRIL 1987

**Wednesday, April 1 (Moon in Taurus)**    You'll be willing to take a secondary role today and let your mate, partner, or associate make key decisions. Focus on home and family, warmth and affection. Don't force any issues regarding security; emotions could rule you today.

**Thursday, April 2 (Moon Taurus to Gemini 8:16 a.m.)**    A lighter, brighter mood finds you in the midst of a social whirl, appealing to others through your sense of humor and intellectual interests. A person met on a journey could be highly attractive physically. Watch your heart! Your lucky number is 3.

**Friday, April 3 (Moon in Gemini)**    Settled conditions prevail, allowing you to catch up on details of record-keeping, balancing your checkbook, and handling joint projects with a solid approach. You'll overcome major obstacles and get praise for a job well done by the end of the day.

**Saturday, April 4 (Moon Gemini to Cancer 6:33 p.m.)**    A romantic interlude depends heavily on physical attraction, sex appeal, and intense heart-to-heart communication. Learn the real story about one who has seemed a mystery up to now. You'll feel rejuvenated by events. Virgo and Gemini have much to tell you.

**Sunday, April 5 (Moon in Cancer)**    In-laws or relatives from a distance pose a temporary problem until a minor disagreement is cleared up. Conflicting life-styles should not be allowed to stand between those who are basically similar. A stubborn person can be easily appeased. Your lucky number is 6.

**Monday, April 6 (Moon in Cancer)**    The accent is on travel, higher education, philosophy of life, and inspiration from a spiritual source. You'll benefit through a temporary escape from everyday problems and "time out" to enjoy concerts, art galleries, or time spent in the beauties of nature.

**Tuesday, April 7 (Moon Cancer to Leo 7:04 a.m.)**    A major career move can be successfully made; be sure you have the necessary education, training, or information you need before you begin, however. Financial backing enables you to meet the competition and gain added recognition. Your lucky number is 8.

**Wednesday, April 8 (Moon in Leo)**    Import/export activities are favored; you'll bridge the distance and language barriers and make gains through keeping a universal viewpoint. If you're working for a cause or ideal, you make major strides today. Aries and Libra people share your feelings.

*Thursday, April 9 (Moon Leo to Virgo 6:28 p.m.)* Your standing in the community depends upon an original approach. You'll have individualistic ideas that can turn away some, but will prove highly popular in the long run. Be bold in standing up for your own beliefs and creative activity. Your lucky number is 1.

*Friday, April 10 (Moon in Virgo)* An older woman or family member proves to be a valuable ally in making your dreams come true. You'll relive the past as you get together for good food and conversation. Your hunches and moods will work for you if you don't allow your emotions to get out of control.

*Saturday, April 11 (Moon in Virgo)* A social occasion brings you in contact with new pals who are clever, brainy, and interested in your creative ideas. Travel and an expansion of views is on the agenda, but don't take on more than you can handle. You tend to scatter your forces today.

*Sunday, April 12 (Moon Virgo to Libra 3:06 a.m.)* This can be a testing time where goals and objectives are concerned. You'll face a choice between solid accomplishment in behind-the-scenes environment or irresponsible escape from duties. Don't be tempted by a bright, but eccentric pal who wants to talk.

*Monday, April 13 (Moon Eclipsed in Libra 9:31 p.m.)* A conflict could arise between you and co-workers or daily associates. The urge to confide personal information to associates is not wise;

analyze data on your own and make the necessary adjustments. A Virgo is in the picture. Your lucky number is 5.

**Tuesday, April 14 (Full Moon Libra to Scorpio 8:41 a.m.)**     You'll emerge from an aura of secrecy to a more open, gracious attitude towards others during this full moon. Don't allow duties to family members or friends to keep you from sprucing up and looking your best. Much depends upon the appearance you make—look in the mirror!

**Wednesday, April 15 (Moon in Scorpio)**     The accent is on the image you present rather than your actual presence. You'll work best from behind-the-scenes, dealing with films, television, or literary imagination. You'll want to escape crowds in spite of a desire to shine before the public. Your lucky number is 7.

**Thursday, April 16 (Moon Scorpio to Sagittarius 12:02 p.m.)**     Nothing occurs halfway on this power-play day. Your business sense will be sharp, enabling you to ask for what you want and get it! Prestige, income, and romance can be advanced by an attitude of responsibility and commitment. A Capricorn supports your ideas.

**Friday, April 17 (Moon in Sagittarius)**     Give free rein to your altruistic impulses; you'll have vision and ideas to help those less fortunate than yourself, gathering resources or cash to aid the needy. Clear out closets and drawers. It's time to get rid of items you no longer need.

*Saturday, April 18 (Moon Sagittarius to Capricorn 2:21 p.m.)* A clever new idea will be a money-maker. Don't hesitate to promote it in an unorthodox, but effective manner. Your personal charm draws others to you today, including a romantic partner who wants to buy expensive gifts for you. Your lucky number is 1.

*Sunday, April 19 (Moon in Capricorn)* A quiet day at home with close family members and other loved ones is just what the doctor ordered. You need a respite from too much busy activity and a chance to catch up on family gossip and news. Capricorn and Cancer people gather round.

*Monday, April 20 (Moon Capricorn to Aquarius 4:45 p.m.)* Writing, publishing, and spreading views puts you in touch with fascinating people from backgrounds different than your own. You'll gain through brief trips, conversations, and teaching as well. A Sagittarian has much in common today. Your lucky number is 3.

*Tuesday, April 21 (Moon in Aquarius)* Settled conditions prevail; you'll be content to catch up on details around the home base and build foundations for the future. A solid citizen with a solid proposition will give you the practical aid you require. Cut through the red tape and see the project through!

*Wednesday, April 22 (Moon Aquarius to Pisces 8:02 p.m.)* You gain a fresh sense of security through inspiring words from an intellectual friend. Break free of limitations and restrictions; your transformed views will help you build more solidly for future. A Gemini is involved. Your lucky number is 5.

**Thursday, April 23 (Moon in Pisces)**    The accent is on music, the arts, singing, and a sentimental occasion that draws family members with gifts. Be open to a change of residence or creative redecoration of your present abode. Love and romance are a strong part of the picture; so is a Libra person.

**Friday, April 24 (Moon in Pisces)**    You'll discover the real truth about a love relationship and will be able to see the situation as it really is. Your secret fears will be replaced by greater trust in spiritual sources. You forge a strong link with a romantic partner through shared values.

**Saturday, April 25 (Moon Pisces to Aries 12:41 a.m.)**    Make the most of this high-powered day for business, career advancement, and a leadership role. Those who share your daily concerns will admire you for your ambitious desire to improve work conditions. A Capricorn is in the picture. Your lucky number is 8.

**Sunday, April 26 (Moon in Aries)**    You'll break free of limitations and look for greater creative self-expression in your daily tasks. You gain a new approach, an end to indecision, and rid yourself of burdens that are not rightly yours. Aries and Libra people are in the spotlight.

*Monday, April 27 (Moon Aries to Taurus 7:06 a.m.)* New moon stimulates your desire to make partnership work—depend on personal magnetism and sex appeal to cement a relationship. You'll be exceptionally creative, especially in joint enterprises that call for original ideas. Your lucky number is 1.

*Tuesday, April 28 (Moon in Taurus)* You'll be content to defer to the opinions of others, especially older family members who have your best interests at heart. Take time out for rest, relaxation, and an emotional response to life. Younger family members appreciate your sense of humor.

*Wednesday, April 29 (Moon Taurus to Gemini 3 p.m.)* Focus on socializing and public relations today. You have the ability to teach and spread your views. You could meet exciting companions in travels, at social events, and in public places. Optimism is at a high point; don't take on more than you can handle.

*Thursday, April 30 (Moon in Gemini)* There is a wonderful opportunity to consolidate money affairs, improve credit position, and catch up on recordkeeping. A steady pace and attention to details are key ingredients for success today. An Aquarius person comes into your life. Your lucky number is 4.

# MAY 1987

*Friday, May 1 (Moon in Gemini)*    You benefit through long-range financial plans, but leave accounting or bookkeeping to another today. Greater income is on the horizon; much depends on expanding your goals and keeping a positive view of yourself and talents. Your lucky number is 3.

*Saturday, May 2 (Moon Gemini to Cancer 2:39 a.m.)*    Practical, routine duties prepare you for travel, further education, or expansion of present circumstances. Consult timetables, make up schedules, and concentrate on self-development. A pioneering type shows you the way.

*Sunday, May 3 (Moon in Cancer)*    A message from afar brings a transformation of views and fascinating contact with one of a different background than yourself. You'll find romance, ideas, and exciting developments through those who write, teach, or travel. Your lucky number is 5.

*Monday, May 4 (Moon Cancer to Leo 3:06 p.m.)* You'll be especially appreciative of luxury, art objects, and music and can turn hobbies in cultural fields into professional opportunities. Your love of beauty and harmony help you gain recognition and successs today. Libra and Taurus people share your interests.

*Tuesday, May 5 (Moon in Leo)*    You play an important role behind the scenes, directing activities of others but not seeking personal glory yourself. You'll deal with illusion, film, hospitals, or charity projects. Pisces and Virgos figure prominently. Your lucky number is 7.

**Wednesday, May 6 (Moon in Leo)**    This can be power-play day where your career and community standing are concerned. You step easily into a leadership role and are willing to acknowledge the respect and prestige you have gained. Love and marriage add new meaning to life. Watch a Capricorn!

**Thursday, May 7 (Moon Leo to Virgo 3:07 a.m.)** The accent is on fulfillment of wishes and hopes and desires through the aid of high-minded, humanitarian associate. Release thoughts of your past mistakes and take advantage of opportunities for expansion. Aries and Libra help you look ahead.

**Friday, May 8 (Moon in Virgo)**    An entertaining person met at a social event gives new meaning to life. Wear bright colors; don't be afraid to stand out in the crowd; you'll be the center of attention if you display true individuality. Leo is in the picture. Your lucky number is 1.

**Saturday, May 9 (Moon Virgo to Libra 12:29 p.m.)**    Avoid abrupt decisions and assume a more passive role today. Home, family, and security are favored. Secrets will be confided to you about close kin that help you to understand recent events. Show compassion and caring for a loved one.

**Sunday, May 10 (Moon in Libra)**     It's a good day for research, study, and behind-the-scenes conferences. You'll be highly stimulated by intellectual ideas, theories, and people from backgrounds different than your own. Try to focus your energies in one direction and maintain a light touch.

**Monday, May 11 (Moon Libra to Scorpio 7:09 p.m.)**     Confidential business can be attended to with precision and thoroughness today. You'll overcome self-doubts and wishy-washy attitude by sticking steadily to a task. A flash of intuition helps to dispel formerly shadowy area. Try your luck with number 4 today.

**Tuesday, May 12 (Moon in Scorpio)**     Lunar cycle surges to high point, bringing variety, travel, and transformation of personal views. Communicate with an exciting member of opposite sex—you'll discover you've won a heart. You have a wonderful way with words, today; express yourself!

**Wednesday, May 13 (Full Moon Scorpio to Sagittarius 8:41 p.m.)**     The full moon accents relationship differences. You become aware of the need for compromise, tact, and diplomacy in dealing with your partner, mate, or the public. Arts, music, or singing are involved in creating greater harmony. Your lucky number is 6.

**Thursday, May 14 (Moon in Sagittarius)**     An extra amount of psychic perception allows you to avoid a deceptive purchase or transaction. Play the waiting game where money is concerned; accent your spiritual values rather than mundane

·matters. A sensitive, artistic person figures prominently.

*Friday, May 15 (Moon Sagittarius to Capricorn 9:37 p.m.)*    Now is the time to buy, sell, or exchange goods and services. You'll have a practical attitude to a business venture, leading to successful negotiations. A top executive will be open to suggestions about an increase in income. Your lucky number is 8.

*Saturday, May 16 (Moon in Capricorn)*    A big project becomes a topic of conversation in your local neighborhood. Put aside petty personal concerns in the interest of the greater good of all— you'll have verbal talent to reach a wide audience and make an effective appeal. Aries and Libra people play key roles.

*Sunday, May 17 (Moon Capricorn to Aquarius 10:42 p.m.)*    Renewed vitality and a changed appearance attract rave notices from family and friends. A sudden romantic opportunity emerges in your local area, leading to a long heart-to-heart talk. A proud, dramatic individual figures in the picture. Your lucky number is 1.

*Monday, May 18 (Moon in Aquarius)*    The accent is on property, rentals, home, and family. You'll set an excellent hunch about a way to improve your home; Use it! You'll be concerned with security, domestic duties, and good food. Listen to some sound advice dispensed by an affectionate older woman.

**Tuesday, May 19 (Moon in Aquarius)**   A family member can be the key to greater popularity and contact with intellectual, well-educated persons. You'll be extraconscious of appearances and your personal image. People and ideas from afar play a vital role in affairs at your base of operations.

**Wednesday, May 20 (Moon Aquarius to Pisces 1:24 a.m.)**   Development of a love interest depends upon proving yourself through steady application of duties and responsibilities. You're building the foundation for future happiness; be sure it's based on solid structure, not just dreams. Your lucky number is 4.

**Thursday, May 21 (Moon in Pisces)**   The pace of life picks up, providing change, variety, and fresh scenery. A romantic interest is uppermost in your mind; someone encountered at a place of entertainment or recreation plays a special role. Gemini and Virgo people brighten your life.

**Friday, May 22 (Moon Pisces to Aries 6:23 a.m.)** You can smoothe the way at work by using a little tact and cooperation. A charming gift—such as flowers or a living plant—will help set the mood for more enjoyable relations. Show some affection to a stubborn person; you'll win them over.

**Saturday, May 23 (Moon in Aries)**   Surround yourself with music, art, and beauty while you perform chores and tasks. You need to uplift your own spirits instead of reacting to a puzzling situation around you. Be content with your own company; you'll learn much about yourself. Your lucky number is 7.

**Sunday, May 24 (Moon Aries to Taurus 1:39 p.m.)** Follow through on any promise made to your partner, mate, or associate. You'll be asked to take on extra duties and show responsibility, but rewards in both love and money are great. A serious relationship intensifies. A Capricorn person is influential.

**Monday, May 25 (Moon in Taurus)** You'll associate with persons who have "one foot in the future" and will be inspired by their self-confidence and charisma. It's time for a decision to be made about a relationship that was going nowhere. Emphasize love and hope. Your lucky number is 9.

**Tuesday, May 26 (Moon Taurus to Gemini 9:55 p.m.)** A surge of independence conflicts with security of long-term relationship. You'll need to balance your self-interested desires for the good of all concerned. You'll have the creativity to envision new ways of relating, but time may not be ripe for decisions.

**Wednesday, May 27 (Moon in Gemini)** The new moon spotlights intense emotional feelings and physical attraction to a member of opposite sex. Making the first move is not advised; let nature take its course. Follow your hunches where love is concerned, but the passive role is best. Your lucky number is 2.

*Thursday, May 28 (Moon in Gemini)*    There's an emphasis on the mysteries of life, including an occult investigation. You'll have a restless desire to travel, probe, and get to the bottom of an intriguing question or theory. Watch your cash—your current mood is extravagant. A Sagittarius is involved.

*Friday, May 29 (Moon Gemini to Cancer 9:59 a.m.)*    The morning is fine for sticking to financial details, setting schedules, and getting records up to date. Later, your mind expands to broader topics, including teaching, publishing, education, and business transactions with foreign countries.

*Saturday, May 30 (Moon in Cancer)*    Take advantage of a chance to travel, communicate, and reach persons at a distance in a meaningful way. You have much information to impart, including affectionate feelings about one who has been out of town. Your lucky number is 5.

*Sunday, May 31 (Moon Cancer to Leo 10:25 p.m.)* Your family and loved ones play an important role in travel plans today. A long-distance move or delivery of household goods from afar may be on the agenda. An ethnic restaurant could be a good setting for a family celebration. Libra and Taurus people are in the picture.

# JUNE 1987

**Monday, June 1 (Moon in Leo)**    You'll prove yourself through a challenging career assignment. Pay attention to the details; learn the rules before you break them. You'll feel a glow of accomplishment and will earn the approval of one at a top level. Aquarius and Leo people are involved.

**Tuesday, June 2 (Moon in Leo)**    A fascinating encounter with a well-spoken stranger suggests romantic ideas. A business meeting or conference could be the scene of a witty exchange that leads to highly personal conversation. Accept last-minute invitation. Your lucky number is 5.

**Wednesday, June 3 (Moon Leo to Virgo 10:56 a.m.)**    Today you'll be rewarded for professional endeavors. Relax from your fast pace and enjoy your family and friends in a glamorous, luxury setting. Your hopes about a romantic alliance depend upon handling a delicate situation with tact. A Libra will help you.

**Thursday, June 4 (Moon in Virgo)**    An aura of deception or illusion surrounds the goals you set today. Be sure you have not been sold a line by a friend or acquaintance who thinks you are a soft touch. Seek the company of a sympathetic, compassionate type who will listen while you talk.

**Friday, June 5 (Moon Virgo to Libra 9:24 p.m.)** A prestigious person in the business world is ready to back your new, more enterprising plans. You're on a solid foundation now with a real influence over groups, organizations, and members of the community. Capricorn plays a key role. For luck, play the number 8 today.

**Saturday, June 6 (Moon in Libra)**    You'll show humanitarian side of your nature by working behind the scenes today. Take up a cause for those less fortunate or visit someone confined to home or hospital. The key is to draw a line at aiding those who need to learn more independent role.

**Sunday, June 7 (Moon in Libra)**    Your original ideas need further development before you unleash them on the general public. A fascinated romantic partner will be the ideal audience for a try-out of creative role. You'll get what you want through subtle tactics. Your lucky number is 1.

**Monday, June 8 (Moon Libra to Scorpio 4:06 a.m.)**    The lunar cycle is high and your intuition is right on target. You'll express your emotions easily and could slip into an affectionate, nurturing role rather than attending to necessary personal business. Cancer and Capricorn people figure prominently.

**Tuesday, June 9 (Moon in Scorpio)**    The accent is on body image, clothes-consciousness, and an enhanced sense of style. Keep your personal grooming perfect; others will notice. You'll go places and do things with a far-sighted, intellectual type who wants to teach you new concepts.

**Wednesday, June 10 (Moon Scorpio to Sagittarius 11:53 a.m.)**    A routine, detail-oriented day allows you to catch up on odds and ends of financial record-keeping and paying bills. In buying or selling, look for quality merchandise that is strong and durable. Be willing to pay a fair price. Your lucky number is 4.

**Thursday, June 11 (Full Moon in Sagittarius)** The full moon brings tension and discussions over money and spending. You need a new look at financial picture with eye for appealing changes. Money spent on communication or transportation could be a good bargain. Gemini and Virgo have much to say to you today.

**Friday, June 12 (Moon Sagittarius to Capricorn 12:05 p.m.)** A luxury gift for the home could become a conversation piece that draws family, friends, and neighbors closer together. You'll play a leading role in entertainment plans and in beautifying your surroundings. Someone with a distinctive voice is involved.

**Saturday, June 13 (Moon in Capricorn)** The emphasis is on spiritual values, idealistic views, and classes that help you perfect arts, crafts, skills, and talents. You may seem aloof to others because your mind is on perfecting yourself in some personal way. Your lucky number is 7.

**Sunday, June 14 (Moon Capricorn to Aquarius 11:45 a.m.)** A family contact helps you build a solid foundation beneath a new endeavor. Luck comes through property, real estate, rentals, and a community involvement that leads to greater prestige. A love relationship deepens on this significant day.

**Monday, June 15 (Moon in Aquarius)** Rise above the limitations of your family background or regional preferences; you gain through a more universal look at world affairs. An Aries type helps you to envision a more pioneering role in life. A domestic burden is about to be lightened through new methods.

**Tuesday, June 16 (Moon Aquarius to Pisces 12:54 p.m.)** Romantic plans loom large as the day progresses. You'll be in the mood for attention, affection, and dramatic entertainment—and you will possess the necessary charisma to draw these conditions to you. A Leo type is in the picture. Your lucky number is 1.

**Wednesday, June 17 (Moon in Pisces)** Allow for a slower pace and less pressure—sit back and relax. You'll be happiest in creative endeavors that allow you to express warmth, affection, and the passive, emotional side of your nature. Cancer and Capricorn people figure prominently.

**Thursday, June 18 (Moon Pisces to Aries 11:56 a.m.)** You'll put off getting down to work as long as possible, fascinated by a multitude of interests and amusements. Your bright, cheerful attitude, however, will light up your employment surroundings, inspiring co-workers. Your lucky number is 3.

*Friday, June 19 (Moon in Aries)*     Basic, routine tasks finally demand complete attention. You'll have to discipline yourself to review, revise, and bring to completion projects that have been hanging fire. Don't allow a restless chum to talk you out of the careful handling of details.

*Saturday, June 20 (Moon Aries to Taurus 8:09 p.m.)*     Restrictions lift and change in your daily routine is accompanied by some mix-ups and adjustments before your chores are completed. Be flexible to the ideas of one with romantic plans; a last-minute invitation could lead to exciting developments. Your lucky number is 5.

*Sunday, June 21 (Moon in Taurus)*     Your marital status and partnerships are highlighted. You'll be in a sharing mood, ready to graciously let another be the center of attention. A change of residence is under consideration; don't be pressured to make new plans unless they are highly beneficial.

*Monday, June 22 (Moon in Taurus)*     A unrealistic attitude about the object of your affection could lead to an emotional let down if you are expecting more than is humanly possible. Play the waiting game where formation of an alliance is urged; you'll see things in a more realistic light later on.

*Tuesday, June 23 (Moon Taurus to Gemini 4:54 a.m.)*     A love relationship heats up as deep feelings intensify. Your passionate Scorpio nature is matched by one who is fully serious about the future together. Show a willingness to take on more responsibility in both love and finances. Your lucky number is 8.

**Wednesday, June 24 (Moon in Gemini)** Completion of a sale or other monetary transaction will be successful. Be aware of the full potential of what you are offering; a petty view of the current situation could lead to loss. A dynamic individual with an eye on the future plays a prominent role.

**Thursday, June 25 (Moon Gemini to Cancer 4:22 p.m.)** Your personal magnetism allows you to play a powerful role, especially as the day progresses. Put your best foot forward in long-range plans, travel, or higher education endeavors. You can spread your personal influence, and gain the heart of one who lives at a distance.

**Friday, June 26 (Moon in Cancer)** The new moon sets the mood for reflective thinking over your personal philosophy, life-style, and more up-to-date views where family in concerned. You'll hear from an in-law or relative who is traveling with news that eases your mind. Your lucky number is 2.

**Saturday, June 27 (Moon in Cancer)** A weekend trip could be on the agenda as your social popularity increases. The expansion of personal activities is a must. You'll meet fascinating persons who offer you mental stimulation and challenges. Upbeat thinking and a sense of humor will be your "calling cards."

**Sunday, June 28 (Moon Cancer to Leo 4:52 a.m.)**
Thoughts turn to career, recognition, and ambition to get ahead in the world. You'll be more willing to curtail your activities in order to master the current situation. Your prestige depends on following rules and becoming more aware of possible limitations.

**Monday, June 29 (Moon in Leo)** Someone at the top of ladder wants to communicate with you more fully, leading to a luncheon or dinner invitation. There are romantic possibilities if you are ready for a quick change in thinking and plans, including a brief trip. Your lucky number is 5.

**Tuesday, June 30 (Moon Leo to Virgo 5:34 p.m.)**
Your artistic, diplomatic, or decorating talents win you applause today. You'll be more aware of beauty and luxury. An older family member or parental figure is anxious to see you succeed in your current professional venture. A Libra is in the picture.

# J U L Y   1 9 8 7

**Wednesday, July 1 (Moon in Virgo)** A romantic message brings an invitation that allows you to socialize, participate in group plans, and bring dreams closer to reality. Be ready for sudden change of schedule that includes brief trips and visits to close kin. Your lucky number is 5.

**Thursday, July 2 (Moon in Virgo)** Family and community affairs require you to play master diplomat. You'll be entertained lavishly in a domestic setting, but will be asked to solve problems and bring together warring factions. One with stubborn views needs a show of warmth and affection.

**Friday, July 3 (Moon Virgo to Libra 4:55 a.m.)** A secret will be imparted to you by a mysterious individual who is trying to shun the limelight. Be compassionate of the faults of others; you'll have extra psychic perception and understanding. Spiritual inspiration is available; tune in. Your lucky number is 7.

**Saturday, July 4 (Moon in Libra)** A conference with a parent or parental figure brings you the backing you need. Both love and money are favored as long as you act in a responsible manner and wait until later to make announcements of future plans. A Capricorn is on your side.

**Sunday, July 5 (Moon Libra to Scorpio 1:03 p.m.)** Rise above petty personal matters, arguments, and jealousies. You'll comprehend the grand scheme of things and understand a new direction better. By the middle of the day, you'll surge into a high lunar cycle, adding to your personal influence. Your lucky number is 9.

**Monday, July 6 (Moon in Scorpio)** You'll begin a fantastic new enterprise, express yourself creatively in both attire and speech, and attract a dynamic love relationship. This is *your* day to shine. Leo and Aquarius associates are involved in dramatic entertainment extravaganza.

*Tuesday, July 7 (Moon Scorpio to Sagittarius 5:05 p.m.)* Pay more attention to your intuitive direction and less to direct action. Emotions rise to surface, making you extra sensitive to the opinions, remarks of others. You do best in a protective, nurturing role, aiding those less experienced than yourself.

*Wednesday, July 8 (Moon in Sagittarius)* The accent is on generosity, expansion, and fortunate increase in income or possessions. You'll place extra value on travel, higher education, and opportunity for socializing and could overspend in one of these fields if you're not careful. Your lucky number is 3.

*Thursday, July 9 (Moon Sagittarius to Capricorn 5:43 p.m.)* Catch up on routine details of bank accounts, interest rates, and paying bills. You need to organize finances for greater efficiency and become more aware of what is yours to spend. Don't be tempted by a spur-of-the-moment purchase that means little.

*Friday, July 10 (Full moon in Capricorn)* The full moon brings surprise changes in relationship, including talk about travel, relatives, and romantic commitment. Keep your lines of communication open, then be ready for change, variety, and exciting developments in local area. Your lucky number is 5.

*Saturday, July 11 (Moon Capricorn to Aquarius 4:49 p.m.)* A favorable domestic adjustment comes about through change or beautification of residence. A gift of flowers, a luxury item for the home, or merely a warm expression of affection adds to the harmony of the day. Express yourself creatively. A Libra shares your sentiments.

**Sunday, July 12 (Moon in Aquarius)** Your home becomes your refuge and place to "find yourself." Develop your musical and artistic skills and talents; work in the yard or garden where you can be closer to nature. Avoid crowds or parties. Pisces and Virgo people can be good companions today.

**Monday, July 13 (Moon Aquarius to Pisces 4:36 p.m.)** An ambitious new enterprise gets off the ground with surprising success, especially if you're organized, responsible, and businesslike. You'll gain rewards of past endeavors and efforts. A love relationship becomes more serious. Your lucky number is 8.

**Tuesday, July 14 (Moon in Pisces)** Creative expression gains through overcoming your personal ego long enough to work for the good of all involved. A dynamic person with a strong sense of competition will become your ally if you reveal humanitarian objectives. Unselfish plans work best.

**Wednesday, July 15 (Moon Pisces to Aries 7 p.m.)** An affair of the heart is especially favored. You'll express the real you giving others a chance to go along if they choose. Your personal charisma is high, love is strong, and you're set for an entertaining, fun-filled day. Wear bold colors. Your lucky number is 1.

***Thursday, July 16 (Moon in Aries)*** Follow strong hunches where your work, health, and dependents are concerned. You'll focus on security, conservative tactics, and emotions rather than logic. Avoid digestive upsets by not eating while under pressure. An older woman has good advice.

***Friday, July 17 (Moon in Aries)*** Your sense of style is accented; you'll be extra conscious of your appearance and will be aware of the appropriate garb for work to be performed. Contact with a person from a distance helps you to make an intellectual decision about a role in daily life. Your lucky number is 3.

***Saturday, July 18 (Moon Aries to Taurus 1:04 a.m.)*** The emphasis is on public relations, marital status, and legal matters. Don't count on your luck to carry you along. Extreme devotion to duty is needed, along with a willingness to review and revise plans. Aquarius and Leo individuals take center stage in your life. Menudo felt Forum

***Sunday, July 19 (Moon in Taurus)*** Communication is the key to successful shared activities today. The pace will be stepped up, leading to split-second decisions and exciting variety. Let your partner make the major moves, while you watch for the right cues. Your lucky number is 5.

***Monday, July 20 (Moon Taurus to Gemini 10:33 a.m.)*** Your partner, mate, or associate shows extra affection and willingness to treat you in a luxurious manner. A special gift of perfume, flowers, or candy is in the picture, along with an invitation to dine out in style. Libra, Taurus, and another Scorpio are great company today.

**Tuesday, July 21 (Moon in Gemini)**     Investigate a financial offer that seems too good to be true. You'll be extra gullible or willing to believe the best of everyone. You're better off concentrating on spiritual, metaphysical, and occult matters. Pisces and Virgo people play prominent roles.

**Wednesday, July 22 (Moon Gemini to Cancer 10:13 p.m.)**     You'll have all the lucky breaks on your side, but actually love or money success today will have been earned by past good works. Establish greater rapport with lenders, key executives, and a loyal member of the opposite sex. Your lucky number is 8.

**Thursday, July 23 (Moon in Cancer)**     You gain wider appeal through travel, humanitarian endeavors, and pioneering enterprises that place you above the crowd. Refuse to continue in a limiting, confining role or position—make plans now for future expansion. An Aries inspires you.

**Friday, July 24 (Moon in Cancer)**     Romance takes place on the way to a distant destination. You meet an exciting person with a dramatic manner and are won over completely by the magnetism and charisma of this individual. Investigate new directions that allow you to expand vistas. Your lucky number is 1.

**Saturday, July 25 (Moon Cancer to Leo 10:50 a.m.)**     The new moon accents recognition and an opportunity to present your ideas before the public. You'll guide others to greater success through relating your own experiences. A family member or close associate provides a sense of security you need for complete self-confidence.

**Sunday, July 26 (Moon in Leo)**     A social occasion could be the scene of an encounter with prestigous persons who are willing to help advance your career. Don't appear too serious about your objectives—lighthearted sense of humor will gain you a captive audience. Display genuine enthusiasm!

**Monday, July 27 (Moon Leo to Virgo 11:26 p.m.)** You'll be pulled back to reality of work that has piled up, chores to be done, and major professional obstacles to be overcome. Be careful with the details; your work will be scrutinized with more than average care. Your lucky number is 4.

**Tuesday, July 28 (Moon in Virgo)**     A love affair you had in mind develops with surprising swiftness, putting your head in a spin. One who impresses you with witty, creative language will let you know of genuine affection. Be ready for a sudden change in plans that includes a brief trip.

**Wednesday, July 29 (Moon in Virgo)**     A family gathering or reunion is favored, calling for beautification of home and preparation of gourmet foods, special decorations, and a festive mood. An artistic friend will aid you with a creative idea—just ask. Your lucky number is 6.

*Thursday, July 30 (Moon Virgo to Libra 10:59 a.m.)*  Don't feel sorry for yourself if there is temporary feeling of letdown. This is the time to reach out and relate to those less fortunate than yourself. Visit those confined to home or hospital, or participate in charitable activities. Pisces plays a major role.

*Friday, July 31 (Moon in Libra)*  You learn the secret of success but need to work on it without fanfare before announcing plans. Love, money, and greater prestige are on the way if you stick with strong convictions. Capricorn and Cancer people are on the scene. Your lucky number is 8.

# AUGUST 1987

*Saturday, August 1 (Moon Libra to Scorpio 8:09 p.m.)*  Secrets will be revealed concerning your family and loved ones. You'll play an understanding, compassionate role in listening to the troubles of others, helping lift burdens. The key is to show you care. Libra, Taurus, and another Scorpio figure prominently.

*Sunday, August 2 (Moon in Scorpio)*  The lunar cycle is high; you'll be extra perceptive, sensitive, and attuned to the latest glamour styles. You win through projecting a successful image even though your confidence is shaky. An interest in the occult or unusual is accented. Lucky number is 7.

*Monday, August 3 (Moon in Scorpio)*   Good business sense and personal enterprise help make a favorable impression on one who can aid your career. Focus on your appearance, tried-and-true friends, and a relationship that could become permanent. Capricorn and Cancer people are important to you now.

*Tuesday, August 4 (Moon Scorpio to Sagittarius 1:47 a.m.)*   A sale or transaction can be finalized after a long search for the right item. You'll have what you want, including more money, love, and time. Let go of past limitations or narrow concepts. Your sense of values expands to include new ideas. Your lucky number is 9.

*Wednesday, August 5 (Moon in Sagittarius)*   A new approach stimulates your cash flow. You'll profit through originality, willingness to pioneer, and a more dynamic sense of self. A Leo native helps bring out your creativity and provides a romantic opportunity. Get rid of a losing proposition.

*Thursday, August 6 (Moon Sagittarius to Capricorn 3:52 a.m.)*   Follow through on a hunch—ideas are plentiful, especially in a writing project, discussion group, or neighborhood get-together. You'll learn through imparting knowledge to others. A good lunar aspect highlights trips, visits, and contacts with kin.

*Friday, August 7 (Moon in Capricorn)*   A social invitation includes travel, good talk, and a chance to expand ideas and learn something new.

You'll see the future more clearly—make lists of goals you desire. A romantic encounter with a fascinating stranger is possible. Your lucky number is 3.

**Saturday, August 8 (Moon Capricorn to Aquarius 3:37 a.m.)**     A family member is a strong force in helping you get better organized. Focus on security, property values, repairs, and revisions. Show you can make dreams come true through persistence and attention to detail. An Aquarius individual plays a significant role.

**Sunday, August 9 (Full Moon in Aquarius)**     The full moon adds a restless note, drives you to communicate needs, desires, and conflicts. You'll have more freedom, variety, and a chance for a change of scenery, but may feel impelled to rebel against authority figure. Romance is in the picture, so is number 5.

**Monday, August 10 (Moon Aquarius to Pisces 3:01 a.m.)**     The search for pleasure is spotlighted. You'll need to make a domestic adjustment that could include a change of residence. The key is to maintain cordial relations with your loved ones, make peace, and plan entertainment that soothes ruffled feelings. Libra is helpful.

**Tuesday, August 11 (Moon in Pisces)**     The focus is on an affair of the heart, creativity, and magnetic personality. You'll be drawn to remote, romantic locales where privacy can prevail. Don't allow unrealistic expectations to mar a wonderful time. Pisces and Virgo individuals figure in the scenario.

**Wednesday, August 12 (Moon Pisces to Aries 4:09 a.m.)** A responsible attitude is called for in matters involving health, employment, and relations with superiors. You'll know what works and can lead others in a more practical direction. Money and prestige could be imminent. Your lucky number is 8.

**Thursday, August 13 (Moon in Aries)** You'll finish what you start, then reach out for higher goals. A pioneering attitude, unselfishness, and a more exciting assignment are keys to greater accomplishments. Ask for aid from an Aries individual who has already been there and back.

**Friday, August 14 (Moon Aries to Taurus 8:38 a.m.)** A new meaning emerges to current partnership. You'll imprint your own personality, dance to own tune, and show the charismatic side of yourself to a dynamic member of opposite sex. You'll deal with public relations and legalities and find luck with the number 1.

**Saturday, August 15 (Moon in Taurus)** Avoid direct confrontations today—you'll be wise to do more listening than talking. Trust your intuition where your partner, mate, or associate is concerned—you may have to assume a nurturing role. A domestic drama involving a family member figures prominently.

**Sunday, August 16 (Moon Taurus to Gemini 4:59 p.m.)**    The best advice is to play the waiting game rather than plunging recklessly into a new endeavor. You'll be eager for knowledge, information, and travel. Be flexible to the needs and desires of your mate or associate; maintain a keen sense of humor. Your lucky number is 3.

**Monday, August 17 (Moon in Gemini)**    You'll be asked to dig deeper for details and facts and figures where money is concerned. Go along with rules and regulations—by doing so, you may increase your financial potential. Be willing to revise the underpinning of your life to rebuild on a more solid foundation.

**Tuesday, August 18 (Moon in Gemini)**    Some exciting changes challenge your creative abilities and carry the promise of romantic intrigue and fulfillment of desires. Be open to serious talk with your loved one and greater commitment in the future. Gain arrives through the written or spoken word. Your lucky number is 5.

**Wednesday, August 19 (Moon Gemini to Cancer 4:19 a.m.)**    A favorable moon aspect coincides with happy news from your family and loved ones. You'll be able to make long-range plans that could involve a change in life-style or residence. Greater luxury is on the way. Libra and Taurus individuals figure in the picture.

**Thursday, August 20 (Moon in Cancer)**    Today brings spiritual values, escape from mundane details, and possible travel plans. Take a realistic view of a distant location—the grass is not necessarily greener there. You'll develop skills and perfect your talents through a class or seminar.

*Friday, August 21 (Moon Cancer to Leo 4:58 p.m.)* Your ambition to succeed at a professional project is highlighted. You'll be more realistic, responsible, and able to reach goals. Organize your efforts—don't depend on inspiration today. Capricorn and Cancer are your best companions now. Your lucky number is 8.

*Saturday, August 22 (Moon in Leo)* Get ready for wider recognition—be aware of those in power who can aid you in a humanitarian project. Your former limitations fall away as you perceive a new goal. You'll capitalize on universal themes and long-range plans. Aries and Libra people are on your side.

*Sunday, August 23 (Moon in Leo)* A creative new approach to your career yields dividends. If you're innovative, you'll strike pay dirt. The sky is the limit if you focus on imagination, originality, and bolder dealings with authority figures. A romantic prospect is a dynamic, fiery type.

*Monday, August 24 (Moon Leo to Virgo 5:23 a.m.)* The accent is on a passive role and lucky hunches. Friends, groups, and organizations help you reach your goals if you go along with their plans. You'll learn by sharing knowledge with those less experienced in your field of expertise. Your lucky number is 2.

**Tuesday, August 25 (Moon in Virgo)** Your popularity increases, you'll have more time for social events, and a wish comes true regarding travel. A witty, versatile attitude is best; leave depression, doubts, and fears behind. A new friend is in the picture, possibly a Sagittarius or Gemini individual.

**Wedneday, August 26 (Moon Virgo to Libra 4:35 p.m.)** Plans will be revised, leaving you momentarily in doubt. Don't look for an escape route—take a more solid approach involving routine, duty, and attention to rules and regulations. Shadows will clear if you maintain a steady pace and firm convictions.

**Thursday, August 27 (Moon in Libra)** A glamorous member of the opposite sex confesses true feelings, leading to a secret meeting, romantic conversation. You'll be astute, perceptive, and able to read into the motives of others. Life will be exciting; flow with the changes. Your lucky number is 5.

**Friday, August 28 (Moon in Libra)** A luxury item is within reach—be patient with a family member who appears to stand in the way. You'll win with diplomacy and sweet words. Stay in touch with one confined to home or hospital. Libra, Taurus, and another Scorpio need your attention today.

**Saturday, August 29 (Moon Libra to Scorpio 1:49 a.m.)** The lunar cycle is high, giving you an extra edge where intuition and timing are concerned. You'll play a glamor role, but may not be as confident as you look. See a romantic prospect without rose-colored glasses. You may only be in love with love.

**Sunday, August 30 (Moon in Scorpio)** You'll have enterprise, daring, and power on your side, especially if you make the first move in an ambitous project. The emphasis is on money, love, and a more successful role in the community. Nothing occurs halfway on this significant day. Your lucky number is 8.

**Monday, August 31 (Moon Scorpio to Sagittarius 8:24 a.m.)** Completion of a current project leads to new opportunities for greater gain. Lift your vision, see beyond the present moment. Let go of the burden that was not rightly yours in the first place. Keep your credit rating in order; pay bills on time. An Aries is in the picture.

# SEPTEMBER 1987

**Tuesday, September 1 (Moon in Sagittarius)** The conservative financial course is best; don't risk money on a project that seems too good to be true. Insist on clarification of terms and all agreements in writing. Avoid shoddy workmanship or poor-quality merchandise. Pisces is important to you now.

**Wednesday, September 2 (Moon Sagittarius to Capricorn 12:04 p.m.)** You'll have the opportunity to elevate yourself in the community in a leadership role. The information you need is available—a phone call or brief trip untangles red tape. A serious relationship gets under way. Capricorn and Cancer people play key roles. Your lucky number is 8.

**Thursday, September 3 (Moon in Capricorn)** The encouragement you need will be offered by an aggressive person who suggests new directions. A limiting situation in your local area will soon be surmounted. New hope is on the horizon regarding love, travel, and a humanitarian venture. Avoid pettiness!

**Friday, September 4 (Moon Capricorn to Aquarius 1:22 p.m.)** An original method of self-expression gains you applause, new contacts, and success in a new venture. Accent individualism, independence, and greater freedom of choice. A property deal will go through as planned; you're on firm ground. Your lucky number is 1.

**Saturday, September 5 (Moon in Aquarius)** A family gathering gives you the chance to relax, enjoy life, and assume a more passive role. You'll reach a greater understanding with close kin if you listen more than you talk. Security needs will be met. Cancer and Capricorn people are communicative.

**Sunday, September 6 (Moon Aquarius to Pisces 1:37 p.m.)** The spotlight is on humor, versatility, and greater confidence in the future. A feeling of being confined is only temporary. A long-distance call or communication brings fascinating news about a family member. A fast-talking person keeps you on the alert.

**Monday, September 7 (Full Moon in Pisces)** The full moon accents love, creativity, and a conflict over play verses duty. A loved one has different ideas about how to spend time, drawing you away from necessary work. The accent is on rebuilding and revision as a solution. Your lucky number is 4.

**Tuesday, September 8 (Moon Pisces to Aries 2:34 p.m.)** Your creative juices flow, romance blossoms, and you enjoy entertainment that stimulates your mind as well as your physical senses. A quick-thinking member of the opposite sex provides change, variety, and a chance for a meaningful discussion. Creative writing pays off.

**Wednesday, September 9 (Moon in Aries)** The emphasis is on health, beauty treatments, and employment of your creative and artistic talents. You'll win through tactful, harmonious methods. A family member with a stubborn attitude could provide a challenge, but the clash can be solved. Your lucky number is 6.

**Thursday, September 10 (Moon Aries to Taurus 5:57 p.m.)** Be alert to clues and secret signals that suggest someone is attempting to let you know the truth. Time is on your side; you can afford to play the waiting game and avoid a direct confrontation. Pisces and Virgos add to the drama.

*Friday, September 11 (Moon in Taurus)*     You'll benefit through partnerships and long-term goals. A romantic member of the opposite sex will aid you in your ambitions—but be willing to show loyalty in return. Legal affairs could turn in your favor. Capricorn and Cancer people are supportive.

*Saturday, September 12 (Moon in Taurus)* Today brings a new opportunity for greater self-expression. You attract public applause, win friends and allies, and shed a burden that was not rightly yours. An old stumbling block reappears, but you'll have help in overcoming challenges. Your lucky number is 9.

*Sunday, September 13 (Moon Taurus to Gemini 12:54 a.m.)*     The accent is on romance, creativity, and intensification of a relationship. Physical attraction and personal magnetism play prominent roles in bringing your heart's desire closer. Keep your resolutions about the budget. An extravagant, dramatic attitude could be costly!

*Monday, September 14 (Moon in Gemini)* You'll get to the bottom of a mystery through keen intuition. Delays may occur concerning finances, but you'll have an alternative source of security. Avoid brooding, worrying, or nagging. An older woman or family member play key roles. Your lucky number is 2.

*Tuesday, September 15 (Moon Gemini to Cancer 11:22 a.m.)*     A sense of humor proves invaluable in a financial matter. You'll get what you desire, then be free to travel, promote, investigate, and gain a wider circle of friends. You tend to take on more than you can handle—don't spread yourself too thin.

**Wednesday, September 16 (Moon in Cancer)** You'll bring long-range plans down to earth and revise where necessary. This is an important period of testing your ideas, theories, and rules you live by. Pay attention to details, but keep the larger picture in mind. Aquarius and Leo individuals figure prominently.

**Thursday, September 17 (Moon Cancer to Leo 11:50 p.m.)** An exciting stranger speaks your language, wants to communicate and exchange ideas to involve you in exciting changes. You'll make a key realization and could break free of tradition. Publishing, education, and spreading the news are favored. Your lucky number is 5.

**Friday, September 18 (Moon in Leo)** It's the right time for artistic expression, career objectives, and greater harmony in relationships. You'll gain recognition for diplomatic manuevers where the top brass are concerned. Those who seem like family to you gather round for celebration.

**Saturday, September 19 (Moon in Leo)** Work behind the scenes promotes your image without revealing the real you. Glamorous ideas can work against you if you lose touch with reality of people, places and things. Avoid misunderstandings with an authority figure. A Pisces shares your feelings today.

*Sunday, September 20 (Moon Leo to Virgo 12:13 p.m.)*    Solid accomplishment earns you favor with a prestigious group. Your ability to make things happen brings your dreams into the range of reality. You'll deal with practical projects, business leaders, and loyal friends. A Capricorn is in the picture; so is number 8.

*Monday, September 21 (Moon in Virgo)*    You'll attract a network of allies, be rid of a losing proposition, and complete a major project. The expansion of your interests is on the horizon. This can include a romantic relationship that blossoms from a former friendship. Aries and Libra people are on the scene.

*Tuesday, September 22 (Moon Virgo to Libra 10:58 p.m.)*    The new moon coincides with a fresh outlook on life. Utilize a group function to display a new you, discover new pals, and imprint your personality. A dramatic member of the opposite sex is attracted and makes no secret of the fact. Your lucky number is 1.

*Wednesday, September 23 (Moon in Libra)* Intuition is sharpened, and imagination increased as you work creatively behind the scenes. Be willing to take a secondary role; let another garner the glory. You have fences to mend, plans to evolve. Take time out for a less active role and more domestic enjoyment.

*Thursday, September 24 (Moon in Libra)*    You'll transform gloom and doubt into positive, upbeat action. Keep your sense of humor, even if temporarily confined or limited. Friends will come to you if you can't go to them. Research into arcane knowledge is favored. Your lucky number is 3.

**Friday, September 25 (Moon Libra to Scorpio 7:30 a.m.)** What was previously in the shadows is illumined as the day progresses and the lunar cycle shifts upwards. You'll overcome a major obstacle, cut through red tape, and transform the opposition into allies. Your satisfaction comes from work well done and projects completed.

**Saturday, September 26 (Moon in Scorpio)** You'll show the courage of your convictions in a romantic situation. Project your personality and looks with bold actions and dramatic entertainment. Words become charismatic tools to convince others of your ideas, dreams, and hopes. For luck, try number 5 today.

**Sunday, September 27 (Moon Scorpio to Sagittarius 1:49 p.m.)** The emphasis is on money, credit, and a luxury purchase for your home or family. You'll spend freely where domestic harmony is concerned—and profit from love returned. Rebeautification of home could become a major project now. A Libra offers wonderful suggestions.

**Monday, September 28 (Moon in Sagittarius)** Think twice before making a financial decision. You'll be more in tune with spiritual values, artistic ideas, and compassion for the underdog. Watch your valuables, especially in transit—you could be forgetful today. Pisces and Virgo people play key roles.

*Tuesday, September 29 (Moon Sagittarius to Capricorn 6:08 p.m.)*    The money picture brightens as you accept more responsibility. You'll gain rewards of past endeavors. An authority figure who seemed indifferent will be ready to back you in an important endeavor. A Capricorn is on the scene. Your lucky number is 8.

*Wednesday, September 30 (Moon in Capricorn)* Communication with relatives and neighbors takes on new meaning. You're in a generous mood, ready to dismiss hate and emphasize love and hope. You'll touch the hearts of many rather than appeal to the petty wants of a few. Aries and Libra people are involved.

# OCTOBER 1987

*Thursday, October 1 (Moon capricorn to Aquarius 8:51 a.m.)*    You receive a favorable response to a recent inquiry regarding business, property, or emotional commitment. Your past efforts win rewards—be ready to confer with an authority figure who has answers you need. Capricorn and Cancer people are on your side today.

*Friday, October 2 (Moon in Aquarius)*    You'll complete an important project today. Family members are on your side and property matter will be settled harmoniously. Let go of old hurts, wounds, and resentments and look to a brighter future.

Aries and Libra people play key roles. Your lucky number is 9.

**Saturday, October 3 (Moon Aquarius to Pisces 10:39 p.m.)**    You shake off the old and begin building for the future. You'll have greater freedom, independence, and renewed vitality. Grab an opportunity to get in on "ground floor" of a new venture. Someone with romantic ideas wants to meet you.

**Sunday, October 4 (Moon in Pisces)**    Avoid abrupt decisions where an affair of the heart is concerned. You'll need time, patience, and a calmer emotional outlook to iron this out. An older woman or loyal family member is on hand, will feed and reassure you, helping to rebuild your confidence. Your lucky number is 2.

**Monday, October 5 (Moon in Pisces)**    Your optimism surges upward, creativity is high, and you're in the mood for an intriguing adventure. An intellectual member of the opposite sex finds your mind delightful and wants to wine and dine you and spur you on. Some exciting entertainment is in store for you later today.

**Tuesday, October 6 (Moon Pisces to Aries 12:35 a.m.—Eclipse at 11:12 p.m.)**    Work, humdrum details, and a challenging obstacle to be overcome occupy you today. You'll win through keeping a steady pace, a determined effort, and your ability to follow rules and regulations. Your co-workers can be transformed into enthusiastic supporters; just stick to the job!

**Wednesday, October 7 (Full Moon in Aries)**
Changes occur in rapid succession at work. You welcome variety, but are challenged by the full moon excitement in the air. Your best route is to talk it out with one who is restless and impatient. Later, say yes to an unexpected date with your romantic partner.

**Thursday, October 8 (Moon Aries to Taurus 3:57 a.m.)** Marital status, partnerships, and legal affairs are highlighted today. You'll need tact, patience, and a charming manner to untangle the situation. Be willing to listen more than talk; let another make the key decisions. A Libra is involved. Your lucky number is 6.

**Friday, October 9 (Moon in Taurus)** See people, places, and relationships as they actually are—foggy thinking could put another on a pedestal which isn't merited. Escapist activities won't help. Be willing to maintain a low profile and play the waiting game. Pisces is in a key role.

**Saturday, October 10 (Moon Taurus to Gemini 10:03 a.m.)** Your business sense picks up; you confer with a partner, then make an enterprising money move. The time is ripe for an intensified relationship, physical gratification, and promises about the future. Capricorn and Cancer share your day. The lucky number is 8.

**Sunday, October 11 (Moon in Gemini)** You take stock of your possessions, desires, and ambitions and make a move to clear your life of time-wasting situations. Your financial success depends on seeing the big picture rather than small, petty problems. A sharp, perceptive, aggressive person aids you.

**Monday, October 12 (Moon Gemini to Cancer 7:31 p.m.)** A revived sense of yourself energizes you; you're ready for new beginnings. You dramatize yourself and your deep emotions to one who can grant you love, money, or a fresh start in life. Be ready for a major transformation. Leo and Aquarius people get your attention. Your lucky number is 1.

**Tuesday, October 13 (Moon in Cancer)** Focus on in-laws, relatives at a distance, and possible travel plans. You need patience, time and diplomacy to set your long-range plans in motion. Don't give up too soon; play the waiting game. You're in the mood for family, security, and an exercise of your imagination.

**Wednesday, October 14 (Moon in Cancer)** Your intellectual curiosity is spurred—you travel, investigate, and probe into opinions and life-styles. A fascinating stranger sees you as a challenge and is intrigued by your humor, optimism, facts, and figures. Don't scatter your forces. Your lucky number is 3.

**Thursday, October 15 (Moon Cancer to Leo 7:34 a.m.)** A solid executive type has an eye on you and wants to see if you can deliver under pressure. Stick to the job—don't be tempted to take side trips. A good time can come later; you're building your reputation now. Aquarius and Leo are important to you today.

**Friday, October 16 (Moon in Leo)**    Creative thinking and a written document lead to greater prestige and recognition. You'll be magnetic, verbal, and highly attractive to the opposite sex. State your case, let others know what you think. Virgo and Gemini people are interested.

**Saturday, October 17 (Moon Leo to Virgo 8:06 p.m.)**    A parental figure demands devotion, loyalty, and more of your time. Concentrate on harmonizing a domestic situation. Flowers, a luxury item, and gourmet foods will help set the mood. Display politeness and tact to family members. Your lucky number is 6.

**Sunday, October 18 (Moon in Virgo)**    You work behind the scenes with a group, club, or circle of friends. You feel special, remote from the crowd and can actually play the role of the power behind the throne. Your emotions run deep. You're drawn to humanitarian causes and have compassion for the underdog.

**Monday, October 19 (Moon in Virgo)**    Long-range goals are in the spotlight, including love, marriage, and greater business success. An aura of responsibility surrounds you, leading a prestigious person to offer help. You'll be good at selling, promoting, and organizing. A Capricorn plays a key role.

*Tuesday, October 20 (Moon Virgo to Libra)*
Erase your fears, doubts, and restricting thoughts—
you'll have an opportunity to move beyond your
current limitations. A universal viewpoint wins, so
does an association with people who are pioneers.
Charity work yields results. For luck, play number
9.

*Wednesday, October 21 (Moon in Libra)*   A
secret will be revealed about romance; your creativity will blossom. A dynamic member of the
opposite sex is involved in a backstage affair. The
key is to throw light on the dark areas and get off
to a new start. Leo and Aquarius people intrigue
you.

*Thursday, October 22 (Moon Libra to Scorpio
2:42 p.m.)*   The new moon accents intuition,
feelings, preparation for a new family role. You'll
act as a consultant to nurture and aid others and
can become too soft over a sad story. Guard against
rumors, impressions, and moods. Heal emotional
wounds in yourself and others.

*Friday, October 23 (Moon in Scorpio)*   Your
sense of style is accented. You become more aware
of your body image and take exciting steps to
improve yourself. Travel, learning, and humor
are involved in this fast-paced scenario. Be sensible—don't take on more than you can handle.
Your lucky number is 3.

*Saturday, October 24 (Moon Scorpio to Sagittarius
7:57 p.m.)*   A solid approach is called for in
health, diet, and nutrition problems. You become

immersed in details, obligations, and possess the will-power to revise and rebuild on a more solid foundation. Aquarius and Leo people are involved. Avoid extremes today!

**Sunday, October 25 (Moon in Sagittarius)**    A versatile attitude is needed in handling cash, transacting business, or communicating about your romantic desires. You're ready for more freedom, including a brief trip and a chance to make the acquaintaince of a brainy person. Your lucky number is 5.

**Monday, October 26 (Moon Sagittarius to Capricorn 11:33 p.m.)**    Make a luxury purchase for the home today. With heightened artistic powers you choose the right touches for more harmonious surroundings. Money owed you will be collected and the financial picture will brighten. Libra and Taurus people are in tune with you today.

**Tuesday, October 27 (Moon in Capricorn)**    You yearn for perfection, beauty, solitude, and want to escape from the local area. Your ideal romance could be all in your mind. Poetry, music, and imagination are favored—write, create, and fantasize. Seek constructive methods of escape. Your lucky number is 7.

**Wednesday, October 28 (Moon in Capricorn)** Your drive and ambition are highlighted. You come back to earth, take the lead in a neighborhood project, and make solid promises about the future. A love relationship deepens if you're willing to commit yourself. A prosperous individual seeks out your company.

**Thursday, October 29 (Moon Capricorn to Aquarius 2:27 a.m.)**    You'll complete what you started, and envision new, more visionary projects. Evaluate a relationship with a family member; be decisive, not wishy-washy; it's time for fewer restrictions and a more universal viewpoint. Your lucky number is 9.

**Friday, October 30 (Moon in Aquarius)**    Concentrate on home, family, property, and security. You're willing to take a bold step, start a new adventure, and think about it later. You can influence others in a dramatic manner, including your romantic partner. Create a new pattern you can live with!

**Saturday, October 31 (Moon Aquarius to Pisces 5:19 a.m.)**    You slow down, seek relaxation, rest, and the company of younger family members. Expect love and affection, entertainment, and an emotional denouement to a romantic affair. Nostalgia about the past can have a strong effect on the future. your lucky number is 2.

# NOVEMBER 1987

**Sunday, November 1 (Moon in Pisces)**    You gain opportunity for greater self-expression, creativity, and a romantic interlude. You'll hurdle obstacles with ease, break free of limitations, and draw a crowd of well-wishers around you. Look for Aries and Libra people.

**Monday, November 2 (Moon Pisces to Aries 8:40 a.m.)** A fresh viewpoint about work impresses your daily associates. You'll be bold, assertive, and sure of your own methods. Now you can move ahead, begin new projects, and promote pioneering ideas. A romantic associate is willing to follow your lead. Your lucky number is 1.

**Tuesday, November 3 (Moon in Aries)** Focus on diet, health, nutrition, and a more peaceful state of mind. Your emotions could rule the day, if you let them. Avoid being critical, impatient, or too wrapped up in your own feelings. A family member proves to be a valuable ally. Show affection!

**Wednesday, November 4 (Moon Aries to Taurus 1:02 p.m.)** Your mate, partner, or associate spurs intellectual curiosity. You desire to probe, ask questions, and expand your horizons beyond your humdrum daily activities. Be more selective of your pursuits—let your partner make major decisions. Your lucky number is 3.

**Thursday, November 5 (Full Moon in Taurus)** Be content with your routine tasks and necessary obligations and concerns. The full moon tugs you in two directions and adds to temptations to go back on your word or escape rules and regulations. Play a low-key role where your partner or the public is involved.

*Friday, November 6 (Moon Taurus to Gemini 7:10 p.m.)*     Limitations and restrictions ease, and more travel, talk, and freedom of movement are possible. You encounter a lively, mental type who wants to tell you all. Express yourself with charm and tact—you'll be a winner in a public relations project.

*Saturday, November 7 (Moon in Gemini)*     Your sense of duty comes surging to the forefront. You'll be asked to help a family member with a budget, loan, or purchase of domestic requirements. Show you care, but draw the line at making another more dependent. Home entertainment is favored; so is number 6.

*Sunday, November 8 (Moon in Gemini)*     There is a special accent on spiritual values and hidden truths. Your psychic perceptions are acute; you know without being told. You find someone who seems to be on the same mental wavelength, almost a soul-mate. Pisces and Virgo individuals dominate the scene.

*Monday, November 9 (Moon Gemini to Cancer 4:10 p.m.)*     Prestige arrives through publishing, travel, or matters at a distance. Your past efforts are ready to pay off. You'll make practical plans for the future, including a more intensified relationship, and ambitious career steps. You may need further training.

*Tuesday, November 10 (Moon in Cancer)*     You write *finis* to your current project and move to a higher level. A generous, humanitarian philosophy motivates you to seek a cause or group you can help. Break free of petty details; give your mind scope to roam. Aries and Libra people figure in the picture. Number 9 is your best bet.

**Wednesday, November 11 (Moon Cancer to Leo 3:45 p.m.)**   Your original ideas are applauded by the higher echelon. You're in line for a new start, promotion, or renewed contract. You dazzle a member of the opposite sex, attract followers, and show the general public your true talents. Your lucky number is 1.

**Thursday, November 12 (Moon in Leo)**   Nostalgia for the past dominates the scenario. A parent or authority figure wants to talk, reminisce, and share your emotions and feelings. You take time out for tenderness and nurturing. Your family background provides a launching pad for the achievement of security.

**Friday, November 13 (Moon in Leo)**   A witty, humorous streak in you makes a bid for attention. You display knowledge for all to see in a teaching or learning situation. Energies may be scattered, leading you to diversified ambitious undertakings. Be more selective; choose the right project!

**Saturday, November 14 (Moon Leo to Virgo 4:29 a.m.)**   The accent is on hopes, wishes, friendships, and social gatherings. You'll be tempted to go to extremes, but will be a winner through simplifying procedures and taking one step at a time. Be sure your plans are down-to-earth. Your lucky number is 4.

*Sunday, November 15 (Moon in Virgo)* Communication is the key to solving problems, working with groups, getting to the heart of matters. You'll be magnetic, wise, romantic, and could become involved with a brainy type. An affair of the heart has a chance to escalate into a grand passion. Go for it!

*Monday, November 16 (Moon Virgo to Libra 3:48 p.m.)* A domestic drama unfolds, with you in the role of peacemaker. Hopes and wishes are tied up with a family gathering, greater harmony, and a possible change of residence. Confidential information will be revealed that helps you tune into the real needs of a loved one.

*Tuesday, November 17 (Moon in Libra)* You build a fence around yourself in a bid for peace and quiet, a chance to be alone. You need to discover yourself, trim down to the essentials, and learn the real inside story. Art, music, and intuition are favored. Compassion plays a strong role in the scenario.

*Wednesday, November 18 (Moon Libra to Scorpio 11:47 p.m.)* The accent continues on behind-the-scenes endeavors, but the focus shifts to practical, concrete projects. You win the favor of a key executive, know you are on the way up, and act accordingly. Fears and doubts dissolve in a surge of self-confidence. Your lucky number is 8.

*Thursday, November 19 (Moon in Scorpio)* You are in a high lunar cycle, ready to make your influence felt in a wider circle. Petty individuals drop out of the picture, and you meet someone with a worldwide viewpoint, dash, and daring. Express yourself artistically. Write, create, draw, paint, perform!

**Friday, November 20 (Moon in Scorpio)** The time is ripe for a new start, including romance, entertainment, and rejuvenation of your personal appearance. The new moon accents physical charisma, intense emotions, and the desire to remake the world and yourself. Dress distinctively. Your lucky number is 1.

**Saturday, November 21 (Moon Scorpio to Sagittarius 4:16 p.m.)** The focus shifts to money, possessions, thoughts of security. Your intuition is riding high, you know instinctively where to spend, where to save. Accept the chance for greater relaxation and attention to family. Allow a romantic matter to develop naturally!

**Sunday, November 22 (Moon in Sagittarius)** A lighthearted, good-humored attitude draws friends, popularity, a chance to make money. You're on the move, but your mind is not on details—don't lose things in transit or attempt to handle highly technical matters. Your lucky number is 3.

**Monday, November 23 (Moon Sagittarius to Capricorn 6:32 a.m.)** A favorable moon aspect coincides with the need to catch up, settle down, and write letters or make phone calls. Be satisfied with your routine; excitement is not in your best interest now. Review, revise, and rebuild on a more solid foundation. An Aquarius is in the picture.

**Tuesday, November 24 (Moon in Capricorn)**
Today brings change, travel, variety, and visits to relatives in your local neighborhood. You're full of ideas, ready to revise plans, and receptive to a last-minute invitation from a fast-talking member of the opposite sex. Your lucky number is 5.

**Wednesday, November 25 (Moon Capricorn to Aquarius 8:13 a.m.)**     Your deepest need is for peace, harmony, and better relations with family and loved ones. You'll beautify your surroundings and plan a special get-together, and give gifts. A disruptive influence will be removed in time. Libra, Taurus, and another Scorpio are on the scene.

**Thursday, November 26 (Moon in Aquarius)**
Spiritual and family values are highlighted. Your sensitivity is increased, but this only makes you better able to relate to the needs of others. You won't feel sorry for yourself if you count your blessings and show compassion to those in need. Your lucky number is 7.

**Friday, November 27 (Moon Aquarius to Pisces 10:40 a.m.)**     Now is the time for more practical and ambitious plans. You see a chance to benefit through property, family background, or domestic affairs. An authority figure is on your side and will help to get this new enterprise off the ground. Love and marital status are involved.

**Saturday, November 28 (Moon in Pisces)**     Your entertainment plans are spotlighted. Your life gains new purpose and greater meaning, as romance blossoms, new friends appear, and you have a chance to display your artistic talents. You'll put an end to indecision as you gain fresh viewpoint. Your lucky number is 9.

**Sunday, November 29 (Moon Pisces to Aries 2:26 p.m.)** You take center stage in performance. Others applaud your charisma, vitality, original ideas. The status quo is out the window. A personal appearance is dramatic and gains the attention of a wide circle of admirers. A Leo is in the picture.

**Monday, November 30 (Moon in Aries)** Accept time out with graciousness. The family gathers round, and you wax sentimental, talk about the past and place greater focus on diet, health, and nutrition. An older woman has good advice about work, chores, or other duties. Your lucky number is 2.

# DECEMBER 1987

**Tuesday, December 1 (Moon Aries to Taurus 8:06 p.m.)** New approaches are favored in your work and health. You originate, promote, make sales, and blaze trails for others to follow. You'll work with someone you love or admire, finding pleasure in everyday activities together. Number 1 could bring you luck today.

**Wednesday, December 2 (Moon in Taurus)** A slower pace and more dependence on the good will of others is indicted. You work with the public, but in a nurturing, caring way—competition is out of the picture. Your intuition proves a strong ally in affair of the heart. Go with your feelings for the best results.

### Thursday, December 3 (Moon in Taurus)
Travel, parties, intellectual stimulation brighten your day. You'll be restless to do your own thing but may have to play the waiting game. Let your partner, mate, or associate handle the details of technical matters and legalities. A Sagittarius is on your wave length.

### Friday, December 4 (Moon Taurus to Gemini 3:13 a.m.)
The financial picture depends on a dedicated effort and the ability to follow through on a project rather than chasing rainbows. Straighten out joint monies, and figure out what to spend and what to save. Make lists; pay bills. Your lucky number is 4.

### Saturday, December 5 (Full Moon in Gemini)
You fall under the spell of someone intriguing and could undergo a magical transformation. Conflicts exist with the full moon in the skies, but you'll get to the heart of matters through much talk and probing of other's ideas and values.

### Sunday, December 6 (Moon Gemini to Cancer 12:20 p.m.)
Expenses for family pleasures will be covered by a generous person. Be prepared for travel, expansion of your viewpoint, and spiritual revelation. A sense of duty to others surges to the

forefront. Taurus and Libra are important to you now.

**Monday, December 7 (Moon in Cancer)** A glamorous visitor from afar adds to the excitement of the season. You learn to know yourself better by dealing with foreign ideas, customs, and persons. You'll transcend petty prejudice and understand more about religious history. Your lucky number is 7.

**Tuesday, December 8 (Moon Cancer to Leo 11:40 p.m.)** Money, investments, and import-export activities occupy you today. You'll be in an excellent position to make deals with those in power. Merchandise ordered from a catalog or from an advertisement arrives. Capricorn and Cancer people communicate today.

**Wednesday, December 9 (Moon in Leo)** Recognition and career interests are favored. You deal with management level and widen your appeal through pioneering ideas. Rid yourself of petty fears, doubts, and selfish motives—now is time to take charge of your life. Your lucky number is 9.

**Thursday, December 10 (Moon in Leo)** You'll have a chance to prove yourself in a "take charge" situation. This is no time to take a back seat—you have too much to offer, including originality, determination, and the backing of a member of opposite sex who finds you romantically attractive.

**Friday, December 11 (Moon Leo to Virgo 12:30 p.m.)** You'll win your way through diplomacy, rather than forcing issues. Rewards from professional accomplishments flow easily when you relax and allow things to take their natural course. Trust a lucky hunch. An older woman you encounter at a gathering has good answers.

**Saturday, December 12 (Moon in Virgo)** The pace quickens, invitations appear for parties, meetings, and group activities. You'll be in high good humor, sought after, and ready to pit your wits against an agile-minded member of the opposite sex. Travel could be in your plans. Your lucky number is 3.

**Sunday, December 13 (Moon in Virgo)** You make progress with hopes and goals through self-discipline, patience, and the willingness to maintain steady pace. A friend with a solid reputation can be a strong ally, but don't hand over the details to another. Aquarius and Leo persons demand attention.

**Monday, December 14 (Moon Virgo to Libra 12:40 a.m.)** A secret is revealed regarding your romantic life. You'll gain more confidence for the future if you discuss matters with a loved one, get to the heart of problems. Don't allow jealousy or insecurity to disturb you; right answers are available. Your lucky number is 5.

**Tuesday, December 15 (Moon in Libra)** Diplomatic family differences can be completely resolved behind the scenes. Seek luxury surroundings, gourmet food, and artistic or musical entertainment.

You'll achieve harmony through seeing both sides of the question; be willing to compromise.

**Wednesday, December 16** *(Moon Libra to Scorpio 9:41 a.m.)*    Psychic and intuitive powers bring the answers you need. An aura of glamour, beauty, and mystery surrounds you, causing others to be reluctant to approach; but they are impressed by your image. Light will be shed on darkness as the day progresses. Your lucky number is 7.

**Thursday, December 17** *(Moon in Scorpio)*    The lunar cycle is high; you're in the driver's seat and will impress others with your stamina, achievements, and the backing of prestigious persons. A love affair intensifies, marital status is discussed, and you make long-term commitments. A Capricorn is in the spotlight.

**Friday, December 18** *(Moon Scorpio to Sagittarius 2:33 p.m.)*    Your magnetic personal appeal makes this a "banner day" if you rise above your petty interests. You'll deal best with big projects, humanitarian endeavors, and people who have one foot in the future. Your life is about to take a fascinating new turn.

**Saturday, December 19** *(Moon in Sagittarius)* You'll profit through original methods and inventive ideas. A dramatic Leo type wants to wine and dine you with romance in mind. Be willing to spend money on your appearance, including distinctive new accessories. Your lucky number is 1.

*Sunday, December 20 (Moon Sagittarius to Capricorn 4:08 p.m.)* The new moon places greater accent on security, savings, and ways to help family members. Avoid abrupt decisions or forcing the issue. You'll need time out to figure plans and listen to the wisdom of your own intuition. Cancer and Capricorn people are involved.

*Monday, December 21 (Moon in Capricorn)* Today brings close kin, neighbors, and an active social life in your local area. A message or individual from afar arrives on the scene, adding to confusion as well as joy. Maintain a light touch, a sense of humor, and the ability to be open to the plans of others.

*Tuesday, December 22 (Moon Capricorn to Aquarius 4:20 p.m.)* You make order out of chaos, catching up with a mountain of details, and overcoming what seem to be insurmountable obstacles. Discard frills and stick to practical methods that work. Time is limited; don't digress from your main goal. For luck, try number 4.

*Wednesday, December 23 (Moon in Aquarius)* An intellectual pal arrives at your base of operations, bringing a breath of fresh air. You change plans at a moment's notice, make brief trips, and are surprisingly open to a romantic invitation. Communication is the key to enjoyment in family relationships.

*Thursday, December 24 (Moon Aquarius to Pisces 5:10 p.m.)* A family get-together is on the agenda, with you in the role of decorator, peacemaker, and diplomat. Your home will be beautified and a disturbing element removed. A luxury gift puts all in a better mood, so does music and entertainment. Your lucky number is 6.

*Friday, December 25 (Moon in Pisces)*   An aura of mystery and romance surrounds pleasures today. You'll be inspired to help those less fortunate, including special visits to entertain persons confined to home or hospital. You are very interested in psychic experiences today. So is a Pisces friend.

*Saturday, December 26 (Moon Pisces to Aries 8:05 p.m.)*   Love, marital status, and greater commitments about the future are spotlighted. You'll have a chance to attend a prestigious theater production or meet persons involved with entertainment and recreation. Your standing in the community is enhanced. Your lucky number is 8.

*Sunday, December 27 (Moon in Aries)*   A humanitarian and charitable endeavor gives you the chance to widen your personal appeal through service to others. You come up with a big, new idea, and are able to promote it on a grand scale. The medical and employment problems of others concern you and keep you busy.

*Monday, December 28 (Moon in Aries)*   Don't expect the status quo—new contacts give you access to job information that helps you make a fresh start. You invent and promote original ideas and express love for another through deeds rather than words. Leo and Aquarius persons are in your life now.

***Tuesday, December 29 (Moon Aries to Taurus 1:37 a.m.)***   A cooperative role is best today. You'll be able to catch up after a period of frenzied activity and will be more interested in domestic concerns than outside activities. Play a waiting game where decisions are needed or let your partner make them. Your lucky number is 2.

***Wednesday, December 30 (Moon in Taurus)*** You deal with the general public in a bright, active manner. This can include travel, teaching, sales, or a witty mental exchanges. You'll have the tendency to take on more than you can handle. Sagittarius and Gemini individuals figure prominently.

***Thursday, December 31 (Moon Taurus to Gemini 9:29 a.m.)***   You'll play a practical, hard-working role in celebrations—and may feel expenses are getting out of hand. Keep your eye on the details, read between the lines, and follow through on what you have promised, but without unnecessary frills. Your lucky number is 4.

*About This Series*

This is one of a series of
twelve Day-by-Day Astrological Guides
for the signs in 1987
by Sydney Omarr

## About the Author

Born on August 5, 1926, in Philadelphia, Omarr was the only astrologer ever given full-time duty in the U.S. Army as an astrologer. He also is regarded as the most erudite astrologer of our time and the best-known, through his syndicated column (300 newspapers), and his radio and television programs (he is Merv Griffin's "resident astrologer"). Omarr has been called the most "knowledgeable astrologer since Evangeline Adams." His forecasts of Nixon's downfall, the end of World War II in mid-August of 1945, the assassination of John F. Kennedy, Roosevelt's election to a fourth term and his death in office ... these and many others are on record and quoted enough to be considered "legendary."